A Dime in the Sand

*A true story of God's light on my path. The path on which **great** and **amazing** things happened.*

by Christine Cobb

Trust in the Lord with all your heart and lean not on your own understanding; in all your ways submit to him, and he will make your paths straight.
(Proverbs 3:5-6, NIV)

WORDTRUTH PRESS

Published in Marietta, Georgia by WORDTRUTH PRESS, a division of WordTruth Services LLC (SAN 920-2811). Find this and other great resources on our website at: WORDTRUTHPRESS.ORG

Cover art provided courtesy of LOVELY EVENTS.

All scripture quotations, unless otherwise indicated, are taken from the Holy Bible, New International Version®, NIV®. Copyright ©1973, 1978, 1984, 2011 by Biblica, Inc.™ Used by permission of Zondervan. All rights reserved worldwide. www.zondervan.com The "NIV" and "New International Version" are trademarks registered in the United States Patent and Trademark Office by Biblica, Inc.™

Printed in the United States of America

ISBN: 978-1-944758-05-9

Library of Congress Control Number: 2019931658

Special thanks to my family, my friends, pastors, caregivers and especially to Mom.

This story is true. Nevertheless, some of the character names and identifying details have been changed for privacy purposes.

A dime out of every dollar in proceeds from this book will be donated to the American Bible Society to provide bibles to the Ntinda Community Church in Uganda. Led by Pastor Samwili Asinai, this church is evangelizing people throughout Uganda and Kenya. Bibles are their greatest need. It is my hope and prayer that these bibles will be a dime in the sand for the unreached people in this region.

Prologue

As humans we often go through our lives trying to make our own paths, decisions and end results. We push and push and try to make things happen in the way WE want them to go. And when our lives don't go as we planned, we wonder why, get aggravated and upset, blame God or someone else.

As Christians we are taught that God has a plan for us and a time for all things. With our faith in Him, we are to understand this and accept it. Human nature can sometimes make this very hard to do. Sometimes God works suddenly and without warning. At other times God works gradually over time so we can see and feel his hands at work. No matter which way, He created us and only He knows our beginning and our end.

Through a series of events as dictated in this book, it became crystal clear to me that God has an inevitable way of weaving us together for His purpose. And His purpose is for love, goodness, grace, forgiveness and most importantly to spread the word of the Gospel.

Through my faith in Him and with an open heart and mind, I could see in hindsight the path that He created for me and for others. The path on which I saw great things happen.

Contents

1
You Did What?

"Mom, MOM! You did what?"

"You let a strange man into your home?"

"You showed him the portfolio of your financials?"

"Oh, Mom, who was he and how did he come to be at your home?" And why would you let a stranger know all about your bank accounts, stock holdings, dividends and even your personal income?"

Mom stuttered and replied, *"Well he came to my church and said he was a ... A ... Oh, I can't find the right word."*

"A financial planner?" I asked?

"Yes, that's it," she replied.

"OK," I answered. *"Did your church ask him to come and talk to the seniors? Had he been to the church and met with you before?"*

"Yes, he came to the church," she replied.

"So, you met him there and other church members have spoken with him too. Is that right?"

"Yes," she replied.

"Well, do you have his name or the name of the company he works for? Did he leave you a business card?"

Mom stuttered and took a moment, *"Umm, I just can't remember his name and I don't think he gave me a business card. I don't see one anywhere. He was a very nice young man though."*

"Oh, my goodness, Mom. I can't believe you did this. This really worries me. I'm going to make some calls to your church and get to the bottom of it."

That's when I knew that Mom was not only becoming forgetful, there was something else going on. She would never in a million years have let anyone know about her financial situation. Not even me. It wasn't that she was overly wealthy, but she had a good portfolio and substantial income for her age that was supposed to help her through her retirement years. I suspected for months that she seemed to be changing in ways that were very abnormal for her. I called my brother and asked if he knew about the incident with the financial planner and he said, *"No."* We discussed the changes in Mom and decided that I should figure out what was going on.

My mother was a strong and astute business woman. She was smart too. She retired from a very lucrative career of selling commercial real estate. Needless to say, she planned well for her retirement.

Mom was a very private person. Living by herself for more than 30 years, she was extremely careful about her safety. By this I mean it was like getting into Fort Knox to get into her house. Driveway gate, security system, barking dogs and always locked doors. No one could get through the gate unless she knew who it was and she was expecting them. She lived about an hour and a half away from my brother and me. It was good to know that she was safe and sound in her home. So, when I heard she let a stranger in, yet alone a man, well, the bells and whistles went off.

She had two lady friends that she was close to and spent time with, Betty and Charlene. I knew them well and was glad that they had each other - the *threesome* they called themselves.

When I heard about this man that she let in the house, my first call was to her friend Charlene. We discussed the incident and she was just as surprised as I was and then began to elaborate on the changes she too had been noticing in Mom. She was having a hard time finding her words and then would repeat one word over and over again in a conversation. She was having a hard time remembering which roads to take when she was driving. She was more argumentative than ever to the point that she and Charlene would have little spats and the threesome would become a twosome for a few days.

My second call was to the church to investigate who this *so-called* financial planner was, his name and what company he represented. The church receptionist didn't have any information, so I dug deeper and called some of the church members who I knew were in Mom's Sunday school class. I was ultimately told that yes, indeed, a man came to the church to talk to the seniors about retirement planning and some of the members met with him. But it was so out of the norm for my mother to meet with him since she already had all of her retirement plans set.

It was time for me to take over Mom's finances. I took a day off from work and we went to the bank and had my name put on everything. Now no one could scheme or trick her into investing money unless I approved it too. Next, I became her Power of Attorney, just in case it was needed. The responsibility for taking care of my mother was beginning.

The goal of this command is love, which comes from a pure heart and a good conscience and a sincere faith.

(1 Timothy 1:5, NIV)

2
Tidbits of Clues

Dimes. Not pennies, or nickels or quarters - dimes.

For months I would find dimes in the weirdest, random places. At first, I didn't think much of it, probably just flukes. But then the dimes would appear more frequently. Instances like, I would park my car in a parking lot, get out, close and lock the door and do my shopping or whatever and when I returned to the car, there would be a dime right in front of my door. I would tell myself: *"I know it wasn't there when I left. I guess I was just too focused on other things and didn't see it when I got out of the car."* I would do my house-cleaning and then later see a dime on the coffee table. *"I know I just cleaned that table and that dime wasn't there,"* I would tell myself. *"Oh well, maybe it was."*

One day I vacuumed the floors and then later that evening a dime was laying on the floor in my closet. *"Hmm, well maybe my husband dropped some change. But a single dime? Not pennies or nickels or quarters, just a single dime laying there all by itself."*

My husband and I went to a restaurant one evening and when we were seated, I saw a dime on the table. I thought the previous patrons must have left it or the waitress didn't see it when she cleaned the table. I could always find a reason for finding the dime. But still, not a penny, or a nickel, or a quarter - a dime.

One day I was in the supermarket and a little girl came up to me and said, *"Ma'am did you drop this dime? I found it on the ground where you were standing."* That's strange, my purse didn't fall over and spill out. I didn't hear it drop on the floor. I took the dime from the little girl and thanked her.

My husband and I are very active in our church. One Sunday we had a church member meeting to discuss spending the extra money from the budget to hire a new pastor. Most members were all for it, except for one person who, of course, was the church treasurer. He stood up and made a speech about why the church couldn't afford to spend the extra money.

"It just isn't in the budget," he said.

Well, me and my big mouth - I stood up and gave a speech too, all the while my husband is telling me to sit down and shut up. I spoke about having faith and if God sent this man to us to be our pastor then we should step out on faith and hire him. The money would come.

After church that day, several of us went to a restaurant to eat. The restaurant was crowded and we had to wait a while for a table to become available. While we were waiting for our table I looked down and right under the hostess stand I saw something shiny. I asked her if I could look closer - and it was a dime. *"Was it put there for me to see or just coincidence that I saw it?"* . . . Not a penny or a nickel or a quarter - a dime.

I went to a self-serve car wash one day and as I was reaching for the vacuum hose, there sat a dime. *"Well someone must have lost it,"* I thought. *"But these vacuums don't take dimes, they only take quarters."*

My husband and I took our annual trip to New York City, one of my favorite places in the U.S. We checked into the hotel and as usual. I was tired from traveling and wanted to take a nap. As I was getting in the bed, right by my foot was a dime. *"The hotel housekeeping person must not have seen it when the room was last cleaned, right?"* Not a penny, or a nickel, or a quarter - a dime.

Just today, as I'm writing this book, I've been fearful, stressed, scared and worried due to slow incoming business. It's been a rough week. As I was driving to see a client for a meeting, I was thinking to myself how hard it is to be patient and to wait. Fear is the *"enemy"* (1 Peter 5:8), trying to overwhelm you. Our God is faithful and has our path already set for us. Just Believe!

It was cold and raining hard, but I thought to myself, *"I've got to do this. I have a meeting and the client is expecting a great presentation from me, so get it together."*

As I got out of my car and walked to get a package out of the trunk to take to the meeting, I looked down and there was a dime! *"Thank you, Lord. You heard my prayers and I will push the enemy of stress and worry away because I know you've got me!"*

I had lunch with one of my closest friends and I told her about finding all of these dimes.

She asked, *"Well, what do you do with them? Do you keep them in a special dime jar?"*

"No," I answered. *"I just put them in my purse or pocket and pass them on with other money I spend."*

She told me about how at times she would see white feathers.

"What does that mean?" I asked.

She said, *"I believe they come from angels and are symbols of protection sent down from loved ones who are in Heaven."*

Interesting, I thought and such a good way to explain the phenomenon.

"But dimes? What could dimes mean? Are they a symbol of something?" I asked her.

She said, *"Well, could be. Maybe you should Google it and see."* We both laughed.

When I got home, I thought about it more and Googled: *"what does it mean to find dimes?"*

Google's answer: *Finding a dime is a symbol or token of completing a good deed or a task well done.* It also symbolizes the circle of life as we humans typically count in tens, such as ten years is a decade, counting age in 10-year intervals. *"Thanks Google, that's helpful information."*

"Now what have I been doing to earn such a

reward?" Wow, that's something to think about. Nothing really stood out to me, just day to day living my life stressed out and always in a hurry to get things done. Too busy to realize that life is trying to send me a message and my life was about to change.

God put those dimes in my path so I will be reminded of Him and to be confident in my faith, myself and my actions.

This is good, and pleases God our Savior.

(1 Timothy 2:3, NIV)

3
My *"Real"* Brother Returns

Our father was an alcoholic and left when I was 11, my brother was 15. A few years later, Mom split the scene too. So my brother was the man in my life while growing up. He and I were pretty close but time moves on and we both grew up - jobs, marriages, children, grandchildren for both of us. And as things sometimes go in families of alcoholics, my brother also became an alcoholic.

He started in his teenage years and continued throughout his life. He was what most people call a *working alcoholic* because he could work his job while drinking and be fine (although intoxicated) and then drink even more on the weekends. I prayed all the time that he would stop drinking, but you know, no one can make a person stop an addiction until they are ready.

In August of 2013, I'd been praying hard for him. I had our bible study group praying and I had him on the church-wide prayer list too. I could just see him spiraling downward and I was really worried about him.

About August 5th, I began to have this heaviness in my heart and on my mind. I couldn't do anything but think about my brother. Couldn't sleep, couldn't concentrate on work, I just had a strong feeling that God was basically sitting on me and I couldn't push him away. No matter how hard I tried. God was *"on"* me and He wasn't leaving.

I decided I had to do what God wanted me to do. I spoke to my husband and said, *"We need to go and do an intervention."*

My husband replied, *"Well, you better be careful. You know he can get pretty angry sometimes."*

"You're right," I said and thought to myself, *"Was he going to be angry, yell, curse, run me out of his house?"* I didn't know. I was a little afraid but I knew I had to do it.

I figured I'd better do my homework first. I called some rehab places and settled with a local hospital who specialized in alcohol addiction. I met with the counselor and picked up all the pamphlets, admission forms and general information. I was ready.

My brother has two remarkable sons. The oldest lives in town close to where his dad lived and where I live. His youngest was on a job in North Dakota. I called both of them and told them what I was going to do. I asked the oldest to come with me and he agreed.

My brother's wife at the time happened to be out of town for a friend's wedding so I thought this was the perfect time. My husband, my oldest nephew and I went to see my brother. It was a Wednesday evening. I called him ahead of time and told him, since his wife was out of town, I would bring him dinner. I didn't want him to suspect what our real intentions were.

When we arrived at his house, we came in and he

was lying on the couch and of course was intoxicated. He was drinking about a quart of vodka every day. Even getting up during the night to take a swig. He was a full-blown alcoholic.

He saw us come in and said, *"Wow, what a surprise. You came too, Son? Ya'll sit down and eat with me."*

I sat next to him on the couch. My husband and nephew sat across from us. After my brother ate his chicken sandwich, I started to talk to him and tell him why we were there. I told him how I felt God was leading me to intervene in some way. I told him how much I loved him and was afraid he was going to drink himself to death just like our dad did. He began to cry and so did I.

I put my arm around him and whispered, *"I know you're afraid. I know because we both saw Dad try to quit drinking several times."*

We had seen our dad go through the withdrawals and hallucinations. It was frightening.

I gave my brother the information I picked up from the rehab center. I explained their process of *drying out* alcoholics. It wasn't a drunk tank. They would put him in the hospital for three days and keep him medicated and hydrated to alleviate the withdrawal symptoms.

I said, *"If you'll let me, I'll stay right by your side the whole time. I'll be with you through all of it."*

His son came and sat on the other side of him and

told him how much he loved him and asked him to please consider the rehab. He told him he wanted him to be around and be sober so they could spend time together. His children wanted a granddad who would love and play with them.

I told my brother that I had already talked to the rehab counselor. The counselor said he had to stop drinking for 24 hours before they would accept him. He literally had to start having the shakes of withdrawal. I was afraid this might be hard for him to do, going 24 hours with NO alcohol.

He looked at the pamphlets and seemed to read some of the information. Hanging his head and with tears in his eyes he said he would do it, but only if I would take him, no one else.

He said, *"I need to think about it a little bit more and if I decide to go then I'll let you know. I'll call you."*

As the three of us left I said, *"I love you and I hope you'll call me."*

That was Wednesday. I waited all through the next day and didn't hear from him. I wanted so badly to call him but knew I couldn't push him. On Friday morning, I got the call.

He said, *"I've got to get some things together and I've asked off from work for Monday. Will you take me this afternoon?"*

As I hung up the phone, I fell to my knees, thanked

God and cried. Then I pulled myself together and called the rehab counselor to tell him we were coming that afternoon.

When we arrived at the hospital, we were greeted by the counselor. I filled out all the paperwork and sat with my brother as the counselor explained the procedure. I walked with him to his hospital room. Stepped out for a minute as he changed into the hospital gown and was hooked up to the IV's. The counselor told me I couldn't stay. I had to leave and couldn't come back for three days.

"Do you need anything?" I asked him before I left.

He said, *"Yeah, hand me that book that's in my bag?"*

I said, *"Sure, what book?"*

He said, *"Just give me the book out of my bag!"*

"OK, OK," I said.

I had no idea what kind of book he was talking about. I opened his bag and the only book in there was a Bible. I was stunned. I knew my brother was a Christian, he believed in God and Jesus Christ as his Savior. As an alcoholic, though, he didn't live that way and rarely talked about it. It was the Bible after all.

I left my brother, went to my car in the parking lot and sobbed, *"Thank you God, thank you. I know your hand is in this."*

Then I called Mom and told her all about what was happening. I couldn't really tell how she was reacting because, at this point, she was having more difficulty finding her words. But I know she was happy.

On the third day of rehab I went to pick him up. The doctor came in to check him one more time before discharging him. I asked him about my brother's health thinking that his liver was probably severely damaged by the alcohol. You can imagine my surprise when the doctor told me he was perfectly fine. No liver damage at all. I just couldn't believe it.

Then the counselor came in and told my brother he could leave, but he MUST attend AA meetings if he really wanted to stay sober. My brother found a sponsor right away who took him to his first AA meeting that very night. He went to AA meetings every single day for one year.

On his one-year anniversary with AA, they asked him to bring someone with him to share in his success and be there as he was awarded the gold coin of one-year achievement.

He asked me.

As we pulled into the parking lot of where the meeting took place, my brother stopped and said, *"Thank you."*

Then he said, *"You know, the night you three came in my house, there weren't three of you walking in. There were four. I'm pretty sure I saw God walk in before you."* God was the <u>fourth</u> person there that night.

So as time went on, my brother stayed sober and

everyone kept thanking me for what I had done.

I would just reply, *"I didn't do it. God and my brother did."*

Unfortunately, my brother's marriage dissolved and he was laid off from his job due to a change in the company. It was not looking good. But he had overcome the fear and regained his faith. He was committed to staying sober. He moved into a small, little house that didn't have cable TV, so he read the Bible from cover to cover.

I can honestly tell you that he knows more about the Bible than I do. My brother now continues to attend AA meetings and does whatever he can to help anyone who truly wants help in becoming sober.

I tried everything I could to help my brother find another job. Knowing that I would soon have to move Mom in to live with us, I quit my job and started my own business so I could work from home and have more flexibility. I was already taking off so much time from work to go down and take her to doctor appointments or to check on things at her house. Ultimately, I hired my brother to help me because I needed his help. So, we ran the business together.

"Thank you, Lord. My real brother is back and I need him for what is coming next."

The Lord will make you the head and not the tail; you will only move upward and never downward if you listen to the Lord your God's commands.

(Deuteronomy 28:13, HCSB)

4
One Seagrove Place

I could tell that Mom was getting worse. I was worried she was getting Alzheimer's. No one in our family ever had memory problems that I knew of. However, my mom was an only child, no brothers or sisters. Her father died from emphysema and circulatory problems and her mother died from lymphoma. That was all I knew and those were the things I was worried about for Mom. Certainly not Alzheimer's.

I took her to see several neurologists and they all tested her. One doctor took me aside and told me I should think about the near future for Mom and how we could accommodate her impending memory loss and eventual cognitive impairment. My load of responsibility just got heavier.

She didn't seem incapable of taking care of herself at that particular time. We agreed that she could stay in her home and she would come to visit me more often. The visits became more frequent and the length of her stay would increase by days each time. I think she was beginning to be afraid to go home and be alone.

It occurred to me that she may really be getting dementia or Alzheimer's and who knows how long she would have before her memory would be completely gone.

One day, during one of her visits, I asked, *"Mom, if*

you could go on a vacation anywhere, where would you like to go?"

She sat and I could see she was trying to process my question and after a few minutes said, *"Well, I guess I'd like to go to the beach again."*

I wasn't surprised. Mom grew up in Miami where the beach was a big part of her life. I thought, *"How am I going to do this now that I've opened the door to this adventure? I've got a business to run and I'm busy. My daughter is engaged and there's a wedding to plan."*

We had a fairly new home but it needed some upgrades. *"Should I really be spending the time and money to take Mom on a trip to the beach?"* Oh, how I deliberated over this - should I or shouldn't I. Then it hit me - this may be Mom's last opportunity to see the ocean again. I would suck it up and just do it.

I called Mom's longtime best friend MJ, who lives in Nashville. MJ is like an aunt to me and we'd talked about Mom and her memory loss on many occasions. Mom and MJ took a trip down to Seaside years before and loved it. They took many trips together through the years.

I asked MJ if she would go and we would surprise Mom. She agreed. They hadn't seen each other in a few years. It would be a great surprise. I asked my daughter to go too.

MJ suggested we go to One Seagrove Place in Florida. She knew someone who had a condo there and said it would be a perfect place. So I made the arrangements. We would go in May, as close to Mother's Day as possible. I told Mom the trip was booked and we were going. I didn't let on that MJ coming too.

The night before we were to drive to the beach, my daughter and I spent the night at Mom's house. She lived close to the airport and we would have to pick MJ up early in the morning. I ultimately had to spill the beans and tell mom that MJ was coming too. She was ecstatic! It was good.

We packed the car and picked up MJ from the airport the next day and headed south. Mom and MJ sat in the back seat together so they could chit-chat. My daughter and I took turns driving. While I was driving, I would try to listen to the conversation going on in the backseat and realized that MJ was doing most of the talking. It seemed strange. Mom seemed sort of disoriented. She was having a hard time getting her words out and difficulty remembering the old stories MJ was telling her.

We got to Seagrove and settled in to the condo. It was a beautifully decorated two-bedroom condo with ocean front view.

First on the agenda was to decide where to eat that night. We decided to go to a wonderful restaurant across the street and began to get ready. Mom was having a hard time getting herself dressed, make-up on and hair done. I went in her room to help her. It really seemed strange. Had she digressed that much? I decided that maybe she was just out of her element and feeling insecure. It could happen.

The next morning, we woke up and were excited to hit the beach. MJ went down early to save the lounge chairs. Then my daughter went down and I stayed to help Mom. But Mom said she didn't want to go down to the beach. I kept asking her why and she couldn't tell me. She just kept saying she didn't want to and had the strangest look on her face. I finally gave in and said, *"OK"* - she could stay up in the condo. I opened the glass doors but was afraid for her to go out on the balcony so I put a big chair in front of the doors so she could sit and look out at the ocean. We were about 5 floors up and had a beautiful view of the crystal-clear waters of the Gulf of Mexico.

I left Mom and went down to the beach. We were positioned where we could occasionally look up and see her sitting there. MJ went up a while later and tried to encourage Mom to come down. A few minutes later, they came back down together arm-in-arm. Mom had her swim suit cover-up on, but no swim suit. I guess she just forgot.

The second day started out early. Mom and I woke up and she seemed to be more 'with it'. Maybe she just needed to relax. She and I went for a stroll on the beach. Mom was a little wobbly so I held onto her as we walked. We walked and talked along the beach with the morning sun warming our bodies and the cool water under our feet and the sand between our toes. Soon Mom was getting tired wanted to go back up to the condo.

As we approached the boardwalk I looked down, I don't know why, maybe to be sure she didn't trip or fall. And as I looked down, there was a dime. A dime in the sand right in front of my foot. It was on top of the sand shining so brightly. Not covered in the sand at all. I couldn't believe it. A DIME!

I picked it up and held it out to show her. *"Look, Mom, a dime in the sand!"*

She smiled, but she didn't know what it meant to me and how I had been finding dimes. We were just happy.

And God is able to bless you abundantly, so that in all things at all times, having all that you need, you will abound in every good work.

(2 Corinthians 9:8, NIV)

5
It's Time

How do you tell someone that they must leave their beloved home, disperse most of their belongings and move to a different place, a place that is not theirs or anything like their home? This was the first hardest thing I had to do with Mom. There would be many other hard times to come.

It was June of 2015. It had gotten to the point where my brother and I were literally taking turns going down to check on Mom. It was time consuming and, at times, very frustrating. We'd have to move our schedules around so we could drive down to her house at a moment's notice. It was taking a toll on both of us.

One day my brother went to repair something at Mom's house. He was like five handymen rolled up into one and was always ready to fix or repair anything. Sometimes he would go just to change a light bulb that had burned out and Mom would freak out about it. I should mention that Mom was a bit of a perfectionist. Her house was as neat as a pin. There was a place for everything and everything was in its place. A burned-out light bulb was just a problem for her.

My brother came back with a funny look on his face and said to me, *"Have you looked in Mom's refrigerator lately?"*

I replied, *"No, not really. Why?"*

He said, *"Well you probably should, next time you're down there."*

Again, I looked up from my computer and said, *"Why?"*

"Well, the freezer is slap full of nothing but ice cream!" he said. *"Any flavor you want. It's right there. No real food, just ice cream. And there's not much food in the refrigerator and what is in there is probably old or expired."*

Sad to say, but the way he was describing it was just funny and we laughed for a few minutes. Then it hit us - she's not eating very much or properly. And what about cooking on the stove. Was she even doing that anymore? Was it safe?

I asked her if she was eating three meals a day and she just flippantly replied, *"Well sometimes I just forget. I eat when I'm hungry and that's all."*

Reason number two as confirmation that it was time to make the move: sell her house and move her in with my husband and me.

I am the luckiest woman in the world to be married to a sweet and kind man. He never resisted at the idea of moving my mother into our home, knowing that it was going to cause a drastic change in our daily living. We decided that we would sell her house then build onto the lower level of our house so she wouldn't have to go up and down the stairs. It didn't seem like too much: add a bathroom, make the dining room larger to be a bedroom and turn the formal living room into *her* living room. That was the plan. She would have her own suite which was right off the kitchen. She could go out on the lanai or out to the backyard with no problem.

Thank goodness again for my brother. He'd had a short stint as a real estate agent years ago. So I put the job of putting her house up for sale on him.

The house sold relatively quickly, though Mom didn't like to have people *trapesing* around her house checking things out. She didn't like it at all.

My brother took care of the sale details and I started going to her house every weekend to go through her things, pack, keep or discard. It took four weeks, in the hot Georgia summer, but we got it done.

Now, I was glad that Mom was such a *neat-freak*. It made it much easier to pack things up. But the clothes . . . Oh, the clothes . . . Closets and closets full of clothes!

Mom did a lot of modeling in Miami when she was in her late teens and early twenties. She was absolutely gorgeous and she was in high demand from the modeling agencies. That's where she got her love of *good* clothes, never anything cheap. Not to mention she had three fur coats.

"What in the Sam Hell do you need with three fur coats in Georgia?" I said to her.

Believe me, nobody wants fur coats anymore. But

she was determined to keep them and they came to my house too.

We were getting close to the closing date on the house so there was nothing else to do but have a huge estate sale. It was exhausting. Mom was taking things very well. I could tell she was sad but seemed to be relieved we were taking over and that she would be moving in with us. She wouldn't be alone anymore. Mom and her two dogs moved in with my husband and me in August.

There is a time for everything, and a season for every activity under the heavens.

(Ecclesiastes 3:1, NIV)

6
Adjusting

My husband and I had been married for 29 years when Mom moved in. We'd been *empty-nesters* for about 10 years and we liked it. We liked that we could walk around the house in our underwear and watch whatever we wanted on TV. We liked to eat out for dinner or just pick something up on the way home from work. I hated to plan meals and cook dinner. But now I had no choice. I had to be sure that Mom ate three nutritious meals a day. It was a new chore that I didn't like, but I did it. I would try to encourage Mom to help, maybe set the table or snap some beans. She tried for a little while and then just couldn't seem to get things right. She was beginning to lose her cognitive skills and she just gave up trying.

Friday nights were date nights for my husband and me and had been for all the years we've been together. But this all changed when Mom moved in. I felt like it was rude to not include her when we went out. I was afraid of hurting her feelings. It didn't sit well with my husband. Friday nights had been for us and us only.

Ah-ha, a solution to the problem! I called my brother. Since I was taking care of Mom, the very least he could do is take her out on Friday nights! Luckily, he agreed.

It was definitely a process getting used to our new

home life. Of course, I was always worried about how Mom was doing and wanted her to feel comfortable and welcome in her new home.

The builders came and construction began on Mom's suite. After months of banging, sawing and painting, the project was complete at the end of November.

Mom didn't feel well the day we moved her things in from the storage unit. I thought she may have had a little mini-stroke or something. She laid in the easy chair and slept. We moved in her bedroom suit and some other pieces of furniture and pictures that she wanted to keep. Then I went to town decorating. Soon I got to the boxes that contained her prized Duncan Royal figurines. Mom cherished those things and had about a dozen of the Clown Collection and the Christmas Collection. She thought they were priceless. Well, as I've come to find out, they aren't. Some of them are still on eBay where I've put them for sale.

When I finished decorating, I woke up Mom and gave her a tour of her new living area. I tried to make her bedroom as similar to the one at her house with all the same pictures, furniture, lamps and bedspread. It was beautiful. She was very happy with all I'd done. It felt a more like home to her now.

My office was originally in what would become Mom's living room so I had to move out. The only place I could move was to the front living room. My brother had a desk on one side of the room and I had mine on the other.

Every day, Mom and her two dogs would sit on the sofa between us . . . all day long. It was nerve wracking. We tried to keep her busy with easy-to-do jigsaw puzzles. At least she was where we could keep an eye on her. Soon it got to the point where I just couldn't stand having my office in the house. The dogs, all five of them now, would bark all the time. I couldn't make business calls with barking dogs in the background. Or the TV would be too loud and I'd have to be the bad guy and turn it down. There was nowhere else to move except to the room above our detached garage. So we moved the office up there. But that left Mom alone in the house. Not the best scenario, however since there was no bathroom above the garage my brother and I decided it would be OK. We'd check on her during our many bathroom breaks.

Everything seemed to be working out just fine, except I was exhausted and taking it out on everyone. That was *not* fine. I'm not going to lie - it was hard to take care of Mom, run a business, take care of the house and the shopping, be a good mother for my now married and pregnant daughter and be an attentive and loving wife. The roles changed between Mom and me. I had to become the one in charge, the disciplinarian, the one to make the decisions and take the responsibility for her well-being and happiness. She didn't like me for it either. At least that's what I thought.

But my brother ... oh, the clouds parted and the sun

came out every time he walked in the room. Mom would light up like a Christmas tree. He was the fun one that made her laugh and didn't take things so seriously like I did. The *Golden Boy* I called him. Thank God I had him back from the depths of alcohol and had his help. God knew this was going to happen and He provided.

Mom was on Warfarin, due to a pacemaker that kept her atrial fibrillation (AF) in check, along with several other medications. This meant finding new doctors close by. I tried to find physicians that were still in her network so her records could easily be moved. I had to find a new primary care physician, a cardiologist, a dermatologist, an ophthalmologist and a neurologist. There were always lots of doctor appointments.

At one appointment with her new primary care physician, a young man fresh out of med school, Mom threw me right under the bus.

He asked how she was doing and she said, *"Oh, I'm fine until my daughter yells at me."*

"What? What's that all about?" I thought.

"Mom, I never yell at you. I may yell at the barking dogs, but I NEVER yell at you." I said.

Thankfully the doctor had seen situations like this before and didn't turn me in to the authorities for elder abuse.

The positive part of setting Mom up with new doctors was the new diagnosis we were given for why her memory and cognitive skills were diminishing so rapidly. We were told she had *Vascular Dementia*. This type of dementia is caused from lack of blood flow to the brain. The one tell-tale sign of this is to have extreme amounts of spider and varicose veins. Mom's legs and feet were almost purple due to the spider veins and lack of good circulation. Now it was all starting to make sense. There is also a greater risk of stroke with this disease. *Vascular Dementia* is very different from just dementia or Alzheimer's. The person with *Vascular Dementia* knows things are changing with their mind and body. Most Dementia and Alzheimer patients just slip into a different state of mind and it happens more gradually. At least, that's my thought about it.

We made it through the holidays, Christmas and New Year. Spring seemed to come early in 2016 and Mom loved to be outside. She would sit in the love seat on the lanai with one dog on each side of her and watch the birds. In Georgia, most people would say they have a back porch. We have a lanai - it is tiled, two levels, covered and faces a koi pond that surrounds a magnificent Japanese cherry tree. In the spring it blooms with the most beautiful pink and white flowers. We would keep a few bird feeders full so she could watch the red birds come and go. I don't know why, but we always seemed to have a lot of red birds in our yard. Mom would sit there for hours, sometimes drifting off to sleep. At times she would stroll around the yard as if she were looking for something.

One day she was walking around the backyard calling for her dog. *"Tolly, Tolly. Come Tolly."* She called for what seemed like 30 minutes.

As my brother and I watched her we realized the dog was in the house, not outside.

My brother laughed and said, *"Well, now we have a new way of keeping Mom busy. It's a new hide and seek game. Tell her Tolly is outside and she needs to find her, but we'll keep the Tolly in."* He always had something funny to say and I sure was glad.

The year seemed to be moving along well. My daughter gave birth to her first child on July 13th. We were elated. Such a happy and exciting time for all of us. A new little girl in the family - my granddaughter. Wow, how life has changed.

For our light and momentary troubles are achieving for us an eternal glory that far outweighs them all. So we fix our eyes not on what is seen, but on what is unseen, since what is seen is temporary, but what is unseen is eternal.

(2 Corinthians 4:17-18, NIV)

7
Call 911

Summer was in full mode in Georgia, hot, humid and sticky, but with the sweet smell of gardenias and magnolias in the air. We all seemed to be adjusting rather well. We were as happy as we could be, given the situation. I'd even been finding more dimes, randomly, here and there. Business was good and I was always hard at work in my office above the garage. My new life as a grandmother kept me busy and I loved it.

One afternoon on August 19th, a date I will never forget, I was in my office. My brother was sitting on the lanai for a few minutes taking a break and visiting with Mom. She was on the upper level of the lanai and he was sitting below. By levels, I mean there is just one big step about a foot and a half high. I was on the phone with a business call and kept hearing my phone beep as if someone was trying to call me, but I couldn't disconnect from the business call. I looked at my phone and saw the text from my brother,

"Come quick." was all it said.

"What?" I thought. *"Was he just going to show me a snake or something? Was he trying to pull a joke on me as he loved to do?"*

I came down the back stairs and walked up to where he was. There was Mom, laying on the floor. The shock

45

that ran through me was like a lightning bolt. I ran to her and tried to get her up.

My brother yelled, *"No. Don't move her. She's hurt."*

"Mom, are you OK? Do you want to get up?" I frantically asked her.

She replied in tears, *"No, it hurts too bad. I can't move. Help me. Oh, help me. It hurts."*

My brother stayed with her and I called 911 as fast as I could.

"My mom has fallen and she can't get up." It sounded just like the tv commercial.

"I'm afraid she may have broken her leg or something. Please come quickly."

I gave them my address and all the information they asked for. I was scared to death of what was happening. I was especially concerned because it was about 95 degrees outside and she was in the sun.

The fire trucks, police and paramedics arrived at my house in about 5 minutes. As they assessed the situation and checked her out, they determined they had to lift her onto a stretcher and take her in the ambulance to the hospital.

Mom screamed in pain as they lifted her and tears began rolling down my face because I couldn't help her.

I rode in the ambulance with her and my brother followed in the car. I could hear Mom moaning in pain.

Every bump in the road was excruciating for her. It seemed like it took forever to get to the hospital.

"Why is this stupid ambulance driver taking the longest route," I thought to myself. *"Couldn't he go any faster?"*

At long last we arrived at the hospital emergency room and she was rushed in. The ER nurses did what they do best and tried to strip her clothes off to get the IV's started.

Still frantic, I said, *"Just cut off her pants. She's got more pants, believe me."*

She was sent for an MRI and the doctor came back with the dreaded news. She had broken her hip. For a weak elderly person, that's not a good thing. We all know the seriousness of this type of injury.

Mom was taken up to the orthopedic floor and put in a room. She had been given plenty of strong pain medicine in the ER so she was out of it. We waited for the orthopedic surgeon to come and tell us what the next step would be. After a long wait he came and explained to my brother and me that she would need surgery for a hip replacement.

"OK." we both said. *"When will you do the surgery?"*

"Here's the thing," the doctor said. *"Your mom is on blood thinners so we can't do surgery until her blood thickens. We've taken her off the blood thinning medicine*

and we will monitor her blood every 12 hours until her blood thickens and she is in the 'safe zone' for surgery. We will keep her medicated so she is not in any pain."

So, we waited. One day and then the next. Her blood just wouldn't thicken. Now I was worried about blood clots especially since she was laying still in the same position for all this time. Finally, on the fifth day, the surgeon said, *"We have to do something. This is not good for her, but her blood really isn't thick enough."* He ordered some blood platelets for her that was supposed to help push her into the *safe zone* for surgery.

"OK," I thought. *"Now we can move on with this."*

But she had an allergic reaction to the blood platelets. She broke out in red hives all over her body, had a fever and her heart was racing way too fast. Mom started to panic and the look on her face was one of pure fear.

Back to the waiting game again. On the sixth day, the surgery was done. My brother and I waited together outside the surgery room. The doctor came out and told us all was good and we could see her in her room soon. Hallelujah!

When Mom woke from the anesthesia, she was, of course, pretty woozy and kept asking us what had happened. She'd been on strong pain medicine for days and really didn't comprehend the situation. The next day the physical therapist came in and the physical therapy (PT) started. They wanted to get her up and moving as quickly as possible to eliminate the possibility of blood clots so she would be ready to discharge from the hospital. On the third day after her surgery the hospital case worker came in with lots of paperwork and a list of rehab facilities. We had to pick one and make plans to move the very next day.

"What? Move her to a rehab center? Which one, where?" I said.

"There are a few close to the hospital," the case worker said. *"You should probably go and check them out and talk to the admissions personnel to see if it's a good fit and they can take her."*

My brother and I left the hospital together and went to the first one on the list. I will call it Rehab #1. We walked in and I was in shock. The place was dirty. There were patients hanging off their wheelchairs and the smell was sickening.

"No way," I told my brother. *"No way."*

So we went to Rehab #2 and it was not much better. By this time, I was scared to death. Everything was spinning. I felt like I was in a bad dream, but I wasn't - it was real. I couldn't put Mom in one of these places. I just couldn't do it. For the first time in my life I began to hyperventilate. I felt like I couldn't breathe and then the sobbing followed. For the first time in his life, my brother honestly couldn't find the right words to say to make me feel any better. We both sat in the car and just looked at each other as if we knew exactly what the other was thinking.

"What are we going to do?" I asked my brother. *"We can't do this to her."*

We went back to the hospital and I made some phone calls to some friends from church who had gone through a similar situation with a parent. Everyone said, *"You should try to get her into Presbyterian Senior Health Center, it's the best."*

The case worker came in again and asked if we had decided.

I said, *"Well I would like for her to go to the Presbyterian Senior Health Center. I've been told it's the best. I just can't put her in those other places."*

The case worker arrogantly replied, *"You'll never get her in there. There's always a waiting list. You need to make a decision and she must be moved tomorrow."*

I stepped out into the hall and said a prayer.

"Jesus, my Lord and my God, I worship and adore you. I believe in you and so I surrender all fears, anxieties and worries into your hands. Lord, I believe in your eternal love. I humbly pray for your help and direction in finding to the appropriate place for Mom. Amen."

Then I called Presbyterian Senior Health Center admissions line. No answer, just a voicemail. My heart sank. I could only leave a message and explaining our situation.

I pleaded to the lady on the voicemail, *"My mom has good insurance and we can pay out of pocket whatever it costs. Please call me back as soon as possible."*

I waited and waited for a return call. Around 5:00 pm I got a call from the admissions coordinator. We talked and I told her the situation. She said she would call the hospital and look into it. She would let me know something as soon as she could. She wasn't sure, but there might be an opening. So I prayed and I called everyone I knew to ask them to pray as well.

The next morning my brother and I were back at the hospital. The clock was ticking and we were still unsure of where we could move her. We were beginning to get very concerned about what we could do.

"Well, I'll just take her home with me if we can't find a good place for her to go. I won't put her in those other places. I just won't do it," I told the social worker.

She, in turn, informed me, *"You can't take her home. She must have 24-hour medical care and rehabilitation therapy. We can only release her if she is confirmed to go to a rehab facility. We'll have to know your decision very soon."*

Then God sent a miracle, at least it seemed like a miracle to me. I received a call from the admissions coordinator at Presbyterian Senior Health Center and she said she had an opening. She had already been in contact with the hospital administration and was just waiting for the paperwork to come over. Praise God.

I ran back in the room and told my brother, *"Go quickly to Presbyterian Senior Health Center and check it out. I'm sure it's OK, but please go and take a tour. Call me right away and let me know."*

I stayed with Mom. He called me about an hour later and said it was perfect. It was the kind of place that I would approve of and that Mom would like. It was beautiful, clean, had a wonderful dining room, physical therapy department, 'round the clock' nursing care and lots of activities. There was even a beautiful lake with a gazebo in the middle stocked full of koi fish and ducks. Mom would be in a room with another very nice lady. Praise God again. Thank you, Lord.

I informed the hospital and told them to prepare to take her to Presbyterian Senior Health Center.

My husband and I went ahead to the admissions office to fill out the paperwork and my brother followed with Mom as she was transported from the hospital.

I could relax a little now and I was beginning to feel better. We'd made it through the broken hip. Now it was up to Mom to work hard with the physical therapy. Everything was going to be OK, I thought. She'll get better and we will bring her back home soon.

But if I were you, I would appeal to God;
I would lay my cause before him. He
performs wonders that cannot be
fathomed, miracles that cannot be counted.

(Job 5:8-9, NIV)

8
Sacrificial Lamb

My husband and I met with the admissions coordinator at Presbyterian Senior Health Center. I signed my name to what seemed like a hundred forms, giving permission for this and permission for that and did Mom like this type of food or did she have any allergies? Did she have a will, an advanced directive, did I have proof that I had power of attorney? Questions, so many questions. I just wanted to hurry so I could go and check on Mom. I knew she was scared and didn't understand what was happening.

As the admissions coordinator moved on with the paperwork, she asked, *"What is your mother's religious belief? Did she attend church and what is her denomination? Our center is Christian-based and we hold church services here every Sunday in the chapel downstairs."*

I answered, *"My mother is a strong believer. She attended a Methodist church near her home before we moved her up to live with us; now she goes with us to our church."*

"What church do ya'll go to?" she asked.

"We are members of the new GracePointe Marietta Baptist Church. It's close to the square in Marietta. It's been my husband's family church all of his life." I explained.

She said, *"GracePointe? Is that the beautiful church on the hill as you approach Marietta from the south side?"*

I said, *"Yes. It used to be the old Crestview church, but we merged with Rose Lane Baptist and now we are GracePointe."*

She said, *"Ya'll have Rev. Price there now as interim pastor, right?"*

Nelson Price is practically an icon in Marietta. He pastored one of the largest churches in the area for a long time before he retired. He is a true scholar of the Christian faith and I'd always admired him. He's written many books and has been a contributing editorial writer to our local newspaper.

"Oh, yes we do and we are so honored to have him at our little church while we look for a permanent pastor," I answered.

She said, *"Well you may not believe this, but my husband and I pulled into the parking lot of your church last week and prayed for your church. We know Nelson Price and we know the story behind your church."*

"Wow, that's amazing," I answered. *"Thank you. We can always use prayers for our church."*

"Well my husband is a pastor," she said. *"He pastored a local Baptist church for quite some time and then we decided to take another direction and move to Florida and start up a Christian-based business there.*

Well, it just wasn't what we thought it would be and we missed home so we came back. Right now my husband is working as an associate pastor at another church, but boy he sure would love to pastor his own church again. It would be his dream come true."

I couldn't believe we were talking about this subject at this particular time. It's amazing how God threads people together so seamlessly.

We finished the mounds of paperwork. Before I left her office, I said, *"If your husband is truly interested in a position as a pastor at our church, then have him contact the church office. I'm not on the Pastor Search Committee, but I'll be sure to let them know to be on the lookout for his call or resume."*

She said, *"Wait, let me give you his phone number too."*

"That's a good idea," I replied.

"Thank you for your prayers and thank you for helping us with registering Mom here," I said.

As I drove home, I called my best friend from church. She and I were on several committees together and most especially enjoyed working together on our Missions and Outreach Committee. We talked a lot about the church, getting a new pastor and all types of upcoming activities we were working on. I believe there is no one more dedicated to our church than she is. She and I were also beginning to be friends with Rev. Price, which to me was such an honor. In my opinion, he was right up there with the Rev. Billy Graham in his knowledge of evangelism and the Christian faith.

"Bridget," I said, *"You're just not going to believe this. You will never guess who I just met as I was registering Mom at Presbyterian Senior Health Center."*

"Well, first, how are you and how is your mom?" she replied. She asked this same question every time we would talk. She is just that way, more caring about everyone else than herself.

"I'll tell you about that later, just let me tell you about this right now," I said back to her.

"As we were doing all the paperwork, the admissions coordinator told me that her husband is a pastor and would love to pastor his own church again. His name is Tim Childers. Do you know of him?" I asked her. *"His wife's name is Debbie."*

"Oh wow, I do know Debbie," she said. *"I attended some of her bible study classes. She is awesome. Oh yes, and her husband is a pastor. Do you think he would really be interested in our church? He would be perfect, just a perfect fit and to have Debbie come too, well that's just icing on the cake. What did you say to Debbie? Did you tell her to tell him to contact the church?"*

I replied, *"Yes, but he's currently employed so I'm not sure if he really would want to leave his job for our church. Debbie gave me his phone number. Do you think*

I should call him? I'm not on the Pastor Search Committee, though."

"Go ahead and give him a call and tell him to contact the church office," she said. *"They'll put him in touch with the person in charge of the Pastor Search Committee. I'll call Rev. Price and ask him if he knows him and can tell me anything more about him."*

"OK, I'll call right now," I replied.

It had been a long day and a rainy night. As I was carefully and slowly driving home, I dialed Tim's number and, to my surprise, he answered. He was driving home too. Thank goodness for cell phones. I told him who I was and that I had just met his wife and would love for him to contact our church. I told him I believed that God was leading him to us. It was just so clear that God had his hand in this.

He said, *"Now hold on. Don't get so excited yet. I would love to pastor another church, but I already have a job and I'll just need to think and pray about this."*

I said, *"I understand. I'll pray too, but I still believe with all my heart that God put you right in front of me knowing that I will lead you to our church."*

"Goodnight," I said. *"Drive carefully."*

And that was the last that I involved myself with Tim and the possibility of him becoming our pastor. I couldn't tell any of this to the Pastor Search Committee since I wasn't a part of it. I didn't want to seem too pushy or that I was trying to influence them. So I let it be and never said another word to anyone about it.

The Pastor Search Committee was going through resumes and interviewing prospective pastor candidates. I heard through the *grapevine* that Tim was one of the top candidates. The Committee made it known that we would have a special guest pastor one Sunday while Rev. Price was on vacation. I hoped it was Tim and it was. He is an excellent pastor, gave an excellent sermon and the church members seemed to like him. To our surprise, after the service, Tim and his wife left and the church held a special meeting to vote on whether Tim would be our new pastor. The vote passed almost unanimously.

I told my husband, *"As terrible as this sounds, I think Mom was the 'sacrificial lamb.' If it weren't for her getting hurt and going to Presbyterian Senior Health Center, we may never have known about Tim."*

I never told Mom that I thought she was the *sacrificial lamb*. Although I did tell her about Tim and Debbie. Since Debbie worked at the center, she would occasionally visit mom and that made Mom feel special. I picked Mom up several times and took her to church with us on Sundays so she could hear Tim's sermons. She seemed to like him, especially since he made a special point to greet her, either coming or leaving the church. Mom liked to feel special and she was.

During the first year of Tim being our new pastor,

our little church practically doubled in size. New members seemed to come from everywhere and new believers were baptized.

It was clear to me that God provided and made these arrangements. It was His plan.

> *"For I know the plans I have for you,"*
> *declares the Lord, "plans to prosper you*
> *and not to harm you, plans to give you*
> *hope and a future."*
>
> *(Jeremiah 29:11, NIV)*

9
First Days at the
Senior Health Center

After we finished all the paperwork and had Mom officially registered, she was admitted to Presbyterian Senior Health Center. We rushed down to see Mom.

When I got to her room, I met her roommate, a lovely sweet lady. She seemed to have similar traits as Mom: stylish, smart and regal in her own way.

"Mom? Mom? Are you OK?" I asked as I leaned over the hospital bed. *"Do you know where you are?"*

Mom had her eyes open, but didn't respond with any words, just a look of confusion. The hospital had sedated her heavily so she wouldn't feel any pain during the transport. My brother had already explained to her that she was at a rehabilitation center so she could recuperate from her hip surgery.

The head nurse came in and said, *"She'll be more alert in the morning. It may be best to let her rest now. I'll call you if anything happens, but I'm sure she will sleep for a while. We'll take good care of her. Go home and get some rest yourself now."*

I kissed Mom on the forehead and told her I would be back early in the morning. I hated to leave her. It was as if I were leaving my own child in a strange place.

The next morning, I arrived at the center early. I

hurried to Mom's room. When I opened the door, I saw her sitting in a wheelchair still in her hospital gown. She was pushed up to the bed table with breakfast in front of her. I thought, *"This is good. She's out of bed and sitting up and eating. A good sign."*

I sat with her and tried to talk to her, but she still seemed as if she didn't comprehend where she was and what was going on. She just had the strangest look on her face.

"Mom, how are you feeling today?" I asked. *"Are you in any pain? Has the doctor come in to see you yet? Have you been able to eat much? How did you sleep last night?"*

She just kept looking at me, not saying a word.

I thought, *"Well, she must still be a little loopy from all the medicine and probably still very tired."*

The nurse came in and told me that normally she would eat in the dining room but, since it was her first day, they wanted to take it slowly. She told me they would begin physical therapy the next day and gave me a list of clothing items that I needed to bring back for her. I wanted Mom to be as comfortable as possible so I immediately left to come home and pack her things.

As I walked down the hallway, the tears just started to flow again. One of the nurses stopped me and said, *"Honey, what's the matter? Your mom will be just fine in no time. We'll take very good care of her. It's OK, Sugar."*

Through the tears, I whimpered, *"My mom is in a diaper. A diaper. Why is she wearing a diaper? She's not incontinent. She doesn't need a diaper."*

"And she's in a wheelchair. I just can't stand to see her this way. It's not her. She seems like someone else," I cried.

As I mentioned before, Mom was always very self-conscious about her appearance. Clothing and make-up were important to her no matter what. And now she is in a diaper and a wheelchair. It broke my heart. I made it to the parking lot and sat in the car with my head in my hands and cried.

I returned later that day with stacks of clothes, shoes, underclothes, make-up, toiletries, pictures of her two dogs and a mirror that she could use to put on her make-up. I tied a little silver cross to the bottom of the mirror. The cross is still on that mirror today. I tried to make her room as comfortable as possible. The rehab process would take from 6 to 8 weeks but, no matter, I wanted Mom to feel as if she was a guest at a resort - not a patient. That's how she would have wanted it too.

But little did I know. I'd never been in this type of situation before. I'd never had a family member or friend in rehab. We were all in for a surprise.

As Mom started her rehab the therapists told me she needed speech therapy. Her cognitive skills were lower on the scale. She had also developed a strange tic and an involuntary jerk that was becoming problematic. It was frightening to her and it caused her embarrassment.

I thought, *"She was declining before the fall, but not to this extent. What happened?"*

The doctor told me he thought the week that she was on the strong pain medication before her surgery and the anesthesia was probably an attributing factor to the significant decline in her abilities.

It made sense, I guess.

The weeks of physical therapy continued and I visited Mom every single day.

Strength and honor are her clothing;
She shall rejoice in time to come.

(Proverbs 31:25, NKJV)

10
100 Days of Alarm

I would go to visit Mom every day at Presbyterian Senior Health Center. She seemed to be doing well with the physical therapy and, to be honest, she loved it. She loved the one-on-one attention. As much as I loved my mother, she was a bit of a prima donna. My brother and I both knew it and decided it was because she was an only child - popular in school and always excelled in any activity she undertook. She liked to hold on to her possessions and didn't much like to share, even with us.

Did I mention she was beautiful? Just beautiful.

I explained to one of her caregivers, *"Now Mom is a bit spoiled and she thinks pretty highly of herself. Don't let her intimidate you. Just go with the flow and make her feel like she's a queen. Ya'll will get along just fine."*

The caregiver laughed and said, *"Well, she's not the first patient to come here with that attitude. We know how to handle it and always treat our patients with respect."*

She was right. They even called the patients by their formal names, such as Mr. Smith, or Mrs. Jones, never by their first name. All of the caregivers seemed to have happy attitudes and were always willing to help or answer questions. They were great with the patients, residents and family members.

"And your mom is one of the sweetest ladies we've had here in a long time," she said.

"What?" I replied. *"Sweet? My mother was anything but sweet. I grew up with her and I know that's not an adjective that would describe her at all. Maybe selfish, self-centered, bossy and a little opinionated when it came to her idea of a different 'class' of people, but not sweet."*

"I don't see that at all in your mom. She truly does seem to be a very sweet and kind lady," she answered.

I chuckled to myself and thought, *"Well, just give it time. She'll soon see the real side of Mom."*

Medicare would pay for 100 days of rehabilitation services - just over 3 months. Mom went to the center in mid-August so by mid-November her rehab would stop and we could bring her home. At least, that's what we thought.

During the 100 days, since I was trying to run my business, help my daughter with her new baby a few days a week, run a home and try to be a good wife, my brother and I set up an alternating schedule for visiting Mom. I don't know why, but we just felt like we had to see her every day (Yup - contributing to her spoiled nature even more). Although we noticed that very seldom did the other patients have such frequent visitors. I took Tuesdays, Thursdays and Saturdays. My brother would go on Fridays and Sundays. On Wednesdays we both took her out to lunch to the same Italian restaurant for her favorite pizza. We gave ourselves a rest and didn't go to see her on Mondays.

One morning during her time of rehab I was woken up early by a phone call from the nurse's station. I could tell it was a night nurse that I'd not met before.

"Mrs. Cobb?" she asked when I answered the phone.

"Yes, this is Mrs. Cobb. Is something wrong?" I knew it was a call from the center by the number that appeared on my cell phone. I had it listed in my contacts and on speed-dial.

"Your mother fell very early this morning and I'm required to report it to you," the nurse said.

Frantically I asked, *"Is she OK? Is she hurt? Do we need to go to the hospital? How did she fall?"*

The nurse replied, *"She seems to be fine, just a little bruised. We put her back to bed and have given her some mild pain medication. You can speak to the head nurse later this morning."*

I, of course, thought Mom was hurt. So I rushed to get dressed and drove as quickly as I could to the center. I got there and went straight past the nurse's station and up to Mom's room where I found her in bed resting.

I asked her, *"Mom, what happened? How did you fall?"*

And then mom started to cry, tears rolling down her

face. She seemed so much like a little child at that moment.

Through her tears she said, *"I, I, just wanted to go to pee pee. I had to pee pee."*

I said, *"Did you press the nurse button on your bed so she could come help you?"*

"Uh huh," she answered. *"I pushed and pushed and pushed. I had to pee pee. I had to pee pee. I wanted to go to the bathroom."*

By this time the nurse came into the room and I asked her why no one came to help my mom.

She said, *"We did come, but she was already out of the bed and that's when we found her on the floor in the bathroom."*

"But why didn't someone come quicker?" I asked.

"Ma'am," she replied. *"We have a lot of patients and we try to get to them as quickly as possible. Your mother was wearing a diaper. If she had to go that badly, she could have just used the diaper and we would change her first thing in the morning."*

"My mother is not used to peeing in a diaper," I snapped back. *"If she wants to go to use the toilet and pushes the call button then someone should come right away."* I was not happy about this at all.

All the while during this conversation, my mother was whimpering like a hurt child.

After the nurse left, Mom said, *"I don't want to pee*

pee on myself. Why, why do they want me to?"

I tried to explain, *"Mom, they just don't want you to get up and fall again, so if you really have to go and no one comes quickly enough then just let yourself go. It's better than falling."*

"But I get wet all over," she replied again through a child-like voice.

"OK, Mom. Let me see what I can do."

A few days later, early in the morning, I'm woken by the same night nurse, with the same scenario. *"Your mom has fallen. This time we found her in the hallway, not in her room or bathroom. She's OK, but you must come in, the head nurse wants to speak to you."*

I hurried, got dressed and went up there as quickly as possible. I went straight to the head nurse's office to meet with her.

"Mrs. Cobb," she said. *"We're having a problem with your mom. She just won't stay in her bed at night so we're going to put an alarm on her bed. That way we'll know right away if she gets out of the bed. Hopefully this will help with her 'wandering.'"*

"Wandering? Mom has never wandered before," I said. *"But OK, if you think it will help."*

The next night, the bed alarm went off and the nurses came running. Mom was out of the bed again. The next night the same scenario and the next night and the next. She wasn't going to stay in bed at night and it was becoming a problem.

I got a call from the speech therapist one morning, which I thought was odd. However, she'd taken a deep interest in Mom and was especially worried about her that day. It was a Monday.

"Mrs. Cobb," she said. "I think you should talk to your mom. She's just sitting in her wheelchair staring out the window and when I asked her what was wrong, she couldn't verbalize anything. She just kept crying. I'm really concerned about her today."

"OK," I said. "I'll be right there." I dropped whatever I was working on and took off again.

I found Mom in a corner, by herself, in the wheelchair and she'd been crying.

I said, "Let's go somewhere private so we can talk. We won't go to your room. How about this little sitting area away from everyone?"

"I don't want them to know," she said. "I don't want them to know."

"OK, Mom. It's fine. Let's go and talk."

When we got to the private sitting area, I took Mom out of the wheelchair and put her on the couch next to me.

I hated that wheelchair and so did she. I didn't know why she even had to use it. "She'd had physical therapy and wouldn't it be better for her to use a walker to build up her strength?" I thought. But I refocused and began to ask Mom about her morning and why she was so upset.

Through her tears she said, *"It's just so loud, every night. It's just so loud."*

I said, *"What's loud Mom - the bed alarm?"*

"Yes," she said through tears. *"And they come and yell at me and push me and tell me I have to STAY IN THAT BED, or else."* She said, *"They yell and are mean to me. It happens every night. Can't I just sleep in my reclining chair? The loud noise scares me and the people scare me."*

My heart was sinking. It was all I could do to hold my own tears back. She was so upset, crying and shaking.

I could tell this was a serious problem. Mom was beginning to get paranoid about going to bed at night. She was so much like a child now and I just wanted to hold her and help her. Even explaining to her why the alarm was necessary and that the staff wasn't mean or trying to hurt her didn't calm her fear at all. Nothing was going to help. The bed alarm had caused an even deeper change in Mom's mental status. Now she was afraid of nighttime.

Mom was declining even more. Her physical strength was weaker, she wasn't sleeping and she had lost a lot of weight. Not that she was ever heavy. She never fluctuated much from her normal 135 lbs. But the stress from the bed alarm caused her not to eat and she was down to 120 lbs.

"I can't let this continue," I thought. *"Mom is getting*

worse, I'm super busy with work and I can't keep running up here every morning. Besides, I don't want her to be so unhappy."

I went to the head nurse and demanded, *"Take that DAMN alarm off of her bed."*

The nurse tried to explain that she felt it was necessary, but I again said, *"Take it OFF, NOW. If she falls, then we'll just deal with it. You have my permission and I'll put it in writing."* She was reluctant, but ultimately agreed. I followed her to Mom's room and watched her actually remove it from the bed.

The next couple of weeks seemed to get better for Mom. She seemed a bit happier, especially because she was getting a good night sleep. It seemed that she could get out of bed and take herself to the bathroom and return to bed, by herself, with no problem.

As I would come to visit Mom, she loved to show me off to her friends at the center and to the caregivers. I think she just liked for them to know that *she* had a regular visitor - *she* was special. One day she introduced me as HER mom. I thought, *"Hmm, strange. Doesn't she know that I'm her daughter?"*

We would walk down the hall and she would wave to someone, rarely remembering anyone's name. But she would say, *"I want you to meet my Mother. She has come to see me."*

I would just shake their hand, smile and say, *"I'm*

her daughter, Christine." Usually the person would just smile back and nod.

Our roles had completely changed now, especially in Mom's mind.

> *So the last will be first,*
> *and the first will be last.*
>
> *(Matthew 20:16, NIV)*

11
Now Until the Hardest Forever

It was November and Mom's 100 days of rehab therapy were up. She was no longer getting the one-on-one attention that she'd become used to and loved so much. She didn't understand when we tried to explain to her why.

I was called to come to the admissions office to discuss the next step for Mom, take her home, move her, or consider long-term care.

My husband, brother and I had already been discussing this and knew that soon we would have to make a decision.

During the time that Mom was at the center, I became very ill with an antibiotic resistant double bacterial infection in my big toe. It was just awful, ugly and painful. After many visits to my podiatrist, she determined through an x-ray that the infection had moved into the bone and now it was truly serious. She sent me directly to the hospital for an MRI and then set up the appointment with the Infectious Disease (ID) doctor immediately following.

My husband and daughter went with me to see the ID doctor. We were all afraid of what could happen - a possible amputation of my toe.

Thank you, Lord. The ID doctor said he wanted to try a very strong broad-spectrum antibiotic that was used to treat infections resistant to typical antibiotics. The medication I was to take had to be administered intravenously every 6 hours for 10 days.

"*Intravenously?*" I asked. "*You mean I have to be admitted to the hospital and have an IV to receive the medicine 4 times a day?*"

"*I can't do that. I have too many other responsibilities. I have to see about my mother, I have a business, I help my daughter with my newborn granddaughter, I have a husband and a big house to take care of,*" I explained to him. "*There's just no way I can stay in the hospital for any period of time.*"

"*No, no,*" he said. "*You will go to the hospital and they will put a port in your arm. Then you will come back here and we will show you how to administer the medication yourself at home. Don't worry, it's not as bad as you think.*"

"*Oh, thank goodness. OK, let's do it, then.*" I answered.

The installation of the port was set up for the next day. My husband was in the middle of a huge project at work and so I asked my brother to take me. I was glad he did because he always had a way to make light of a bad situation. I wasn't scared, at least for a while.

So I started the regimen of treating myself through my IV the next day. I start early in the morning at 6:00 a.m., again at noon, again at 6:00 p.m. and, again, at midnight. It was exhausting. I was also taking care of my new granddaughter so I would take the medicine balls with me to my daughter's house for the noon treatment. The medication had to be refrigerated and thawed to room temperature before I could start the IV, so that meant I had to wait about 30 minutes each time before I hooked up. It took about an hour for each infusion and there were many times, I'd be hooked up and still trying to answer e-mails or phone calls. After all, I still had to work and I tried to keep this whole sickness to myself and not let my clients know. I didn't want anyone to think that I was weak and couldn't continue my business.

I went to see the ID doctor every other day for blood work and to refill the prescription, a bunch of baseball sized medicine balls with lots of syringes of IV flush. I looked like a bag lady walking out of his office each time. My toe was getting better though. Still sore to walk, but it seemed to be healing.

On the 6th day of treatment, I went to the ID office and told the nurse, *"I don't really feel well today. Maybe I'm getting the flu or something. I feel really tired, have chills and I think I have a fever too."*

She had a look of alarm on her face and she said, *"I'll be right back. Let me go get the doctor."*

The doctor came in, checked me out and then said, *"Spit in this tube. I'm going to test you for the flu. I'm going to put a rush on this specimen and we should have an answer this afternoon. You may have the flu and, if so, you'll be very contagious, so try to keep to yourself. Just go home and take your medicine as scheduled and try to get some rest today."* So that's what I did.

The next morning, I received a call from Presbyterian Senior Health Center. *"Mrs. Cobb, your mother seems to be ill. We've called the doctor in to examine her. We just wanted to make you aware. She's running a slight fever and seems to be confused and hallucinating a bit. These symptoms are typical of a UTI, but we will know more when the doctor gets here. Would you like to be here when the doctor comes?"*

My biggest fear with Mom is that she would have a stroke. I was always worried that whenever she got sick, it would result in a stroke.

"What am I going to do?" I thought. *"My doctor said to keep away from anyone in case I'm contagious with the flu."* I didn't care. I rushed up there anyway. When I arrived at the center, I suited up with mask, paper robe and gloves. I couldn't take the chance of getting her sick and I sure couldn't take the chance of getting whatever she had.

The nurse came in and saw me sitting there with Mom, all suited up and said, *"What in the world is going on?"*

I explained my situation to her and then I said, *"But I had to come and see Mom for myself. To make sure she's OK."*

"Honey, you can't be here if you're sick and possibly contagious. You have to go, right now. You shouldn't have come and put your mom and the other patients at risk. Go. Go. Go. I will have the doctor call you about your mom," she said.

I told Mom I loved her and I would see her soon and left.

As I got home, I began to get sicker and sicker. My temperature spiked up to about 104. I had severe body aches, uncontrollable shaking and my heart rate raced well over 100 beats per minute. My blood pressure kept going up too. I was sick and I was scared. It lasted for about three hours and then it would all go away leaving me feeling lethargic. Then I would take the next dose of medication and about two hours later all the symptoms would come back again. The ID doctor called and said I didn't have the flu and I wasn't contagious. I told him what was happening and he was puzzled too and told me to come in as soon as possible. He took more blood for testing and everything came back OK except for my liver and kidney enzymes. He said that was probably from the strong medication. He said to continue to take the medication and stay on the regimen. So I did, but the symptoms continued about every three hours. I persuasively told my husband to take me to the ER.

"There's something terribly wrong," I said to him.

When we got to the hospital, they took more blood

for testing, called my ID doctor and hooked me up to all the typical IVs for hydration and pain. My fever was just slightly above normal and my blood pressure seemed OK. The doctor released me and told me to go home and rest. About the time we pulled into our driveway from the hospital the symptoms started up again. It was horrible, painful and frightening. No one could tell me why. *"What is wrong with me?"* I screamed in frustration.

The next day I received a call from the emergency room administrator. *"Mrs. Cobb, you need to come back to the ER immediately. Your blood is showing an extremely high amount of gram-negative cells and you're very sick."*

I freaked out. I said, *"Have you contacted my ID doctor? Did he tell you that I needed to come back to the hospital?"*

She said, *"No, we aren't required to call your doctor. We need you to come now."*

I said, *"Well I want to speak to my doctor first. I'll call him."*

After speaking to my doctor, he told me not to go back to the hospital just yet. He wanted to look further into my blood work. My podiatrist called and ordered another emergency MRI scan. She thought she might have missed something and was very concerned. So, she set up the appointment and off I went.

I was just so scared. I started to cry. I knew I

couldn't drive and since my brother was there, he took me to the MRI. I was sick to my stomach the whole time I was there, running a low-grade fever. I experienced all the symptoms again through the night. My ID doctor called back the next morning and said he wanted me to stop the medicine for 24 hours. During that time, I didn't have any of the symptoms, I was just very tired.

I went to his office the next day and he explained that it is very rare, but sometimes a patient can become allergic to the medication and he thought that may be the culprit. He wanted to try a different intravenous medicine. I administered the new medicine and the symptoms came back again. I called him and said, *"Doctor, I don't want to take any more medicine. Can we just see what happens if I stop taking it for a few days?"*

He said, *"Mrs. Cobb, please do me one favor and take it one more time so we can truly determine that you have an allergy to this medicine."*

I agreed.

That night about 2 hours after taking the medicine, the symptoms came back and it was about 10 times worse. I laid in bed and repeated the Lord's prayer over and over again. My husband knelt by my side, his head in his hands, praying too. I was having such convulsions that he had to literally lay on top of me to keep me from shaking. After about an hour my body started to calm down.

I called my doctor the next morning and told him

what happened the night before. I said, *"Doctor, I'm not going to take any more medicine. I refuse. I can't continue to go through these spells. Let's just see what happens."*

Reluctantly, he agreed – as long as I would come in every two days for blood work. I was supposed to be on a 10-day regimen. He was afraid that since I didn't complete the 10 days, the infection would reoccur. God worked another miracle and the infection cleared up. I was fine by the end of the 10th day.

Now I just have a *booger toe* as my brother would say.

He teased me and said, *"You know, if you were an Indian, your name could be 'crooked toe.'"* We just laughed about it and to this day, I have a *booger toe.*

During the time I was sick, my brother had to visit my mother. He kept our visiting schedule right on track and, as soon as I was well again, we were summoned back to the admissions office at the center.

"Have you made a decision on how you would like to proceed with your Mom?" the admissions coordinator asked.

I answered, *"I want to bring her home."*

"Honey," my husband said, *"You know your mother needs 24-hour care. How can you possibly take care of her, work your job and do all the other things you do? You are just recuperating from a very serious illness too. And*

remember, we agreed that when your mom became too ill for you to take care of, then she would have to be moved to a full-time care facility."

My brother chimed in and said, *"He's right and you know he's right. She'll be better here with long-term care."*

I began to cry but agreed with them. I signed the paperwork and Mom transitioned from a patient to a resident. She would stay in the nursing care part of the center. I felt like I had just signed her death sentence and betrayed her. My heart hurt more with that one simple act than at any other time in my life.

I cried, *"I can't tell her, I just can't do it. I'll break down and I just can't do it. I promised her I would never do this to her. I can't tell her, I just can't, I just can't,"* I sobbed uncontrollably.

It was a sad day when my brother visited her that Sunday. He took her out to the gazebo in the lake. They fed the ducks and fish and then he told her. I don't know exactly what he said to her or how he went about explaining it. I think it's better that I don't know. That was a hard and sad conversation between he and Mom. I'm thankful to God that He gave my brother strength and the right words to say to her. If you put your trust in Him and ask for His help, He will be there for you to comfort and guide you. I know my brother prayed to our Heavenly Father before he talked to Mom that day.

But I'm glad I wasn't there and I'm thankful to him for explaining to her that she wouldn't be coming home. I know it was very hard for him and even harder for him to see Mom's reaction. She cried and, even though he won't admit it, I'm sure he cried too.

I could only think, *"What would I have done all this time if my brother were still drinking and I didn't have him to help me?"* I lowered my head and thanked God again and asked him to continue to give us strength - we were going to need it.

Do not grieve, for the joy of the Lord is
your strength.

(Nehemiah 8:10, NIV)

12
Holidays ... Just Different

It was Friday, November 18th, and Mom's birthday was the next day. I was on my way to the supermarket, which was just about four miles from my home, to buy a cake for her. That is when I saw the sign (at last). I'd been wondering for months was type of new business was being built across from the shopping center.

TRELLIS HARBOR
Assisted Living and Memory Care
Opening Spring of 2017

Hallelujah! We could move Mom from the Presbyterian Senior Health Center to a brand, new facility four miles from my home. Oh, what a relief it would be to have her so close. We loved the Presbyterian Senior Health Center, but it took about 30 minutes to get there making it an hour round trip for either my brother or myself every day.

There wasn't a phone number on the sign so I did some research, got on-line and found a phone number to the corporate office.

"Hi, this is Christine Cobb. I live about four miles from the new Trellis Harbor facility which I see by the sign is scheduled to open in the Spring. I'm VERY

interested in speaking to you about the facility. I would love to move my mom. It would be just perfect to have her so close to me," I said. Then I explained to her a bit more about Mom's current situation, her health issues and where she was living.

"What a blessing," I thought. "Having Mom close by will make my life so much easier. God, you came through again and right on time!"

The next day was Mom's birthday. The year before she turned 80 and I put on a wonderful party for her. She'd been living with us for only a few months at that time and I knew she missed her friends and neighbors from her home. I set it up with her two friends Charlene and Betty. We planned the party at a restaurant close to where Mom used to live. Betty was very crafty and she was in charge of the decorations. Charlene was in charge of the cake. I designed beautiful invitations with an autumn theme, complete with RSVP cards and mailed to all of Mom's friends. The three of us worked together and about thirty of Mom's friends turned out for the party.

It was a sit-down luncheon with a preselected menu. I curled Mom's hair that morning and she wore the prettiest sweater set with navy blue slacks. She looked beautiful.

I was glad that I'd thought to make name tags for everyone, because I wanted it to seem like Mom remembered each of their names. I knew it would be hard for her and a few times, even with the name tags, she was confused and didn't quite remember who some were and from where she knew them - church, neighborhood, knitting club, etc. She'd just smile and hold out her hand to greet them. It didn't matter. Everyone was so happy to see Mom and she was happy too. She just beamed with joy.

That party was a sweet success. I was glad that we had the party for her because I knew in my heart that it may be the last time she'd see most of those people and certainly wouldn't remember them much longer.

This year's birthday was much different, but my brother and I were determined to make it as special as we could.

By this time, it was getting harder to take Mom out for our weekly Wednesday pizza lunch. She was having more difficulty feeding herself and it had become embarrassing for her. So we decided to have the party in one of the meeting rooms at the center. We invited the three ladies she'd become close to at the center. We invited some of the nurses too. My brother, my husband, our kids and grandkids all came. We had cake and gave her birthday gifts. It was a bittersweet party. Mom had some problems remembering the names of her grandchildren and certainly had a hard time opening her gifts. But she was happy to be the center of attention once again.

And the ladies LOVED my brother. Oh how they would get excited when he would come. The *Golden-Boy*.

The fun, funny, handsome man who would dote on all of them. They looked forward to his visiting days. There were even times when he would kid around and joke with them, making them laugh and Mom would get jealous. He was HER Golden-Boy, not theirs. As I mentioned before, Mom didn't much like to share. There were a few times when Mom would be so jealous that she would just turn her wheelchair and roll herself away from them and pout. It really was sort of funny. Occasionally my brother would visit and bring his dog - an Australian Shepherd he named Bullet. He would walk through the commons area and the residents would just flock to him. He loved to talk to all of them and the nurses too. He's such a flirt, but he had a way of making everyone feel important.

The first major holiday with Mom at the center was Thanksgiving. I wasn't quite sure how we would handle that day. Thanksgiving was Mom's favorite holiday. She'd cook and cook and prepare for days and the whole family was expected to be at her home for dinner. She'd even set up games in the backyard.

My brother would say, *"Mom, we are not the Kennedys and this is not Camelot. Nobody wants to play badminton! Heck the kids don't even know what badminton is."* She would send back a piercing look that only she could give and we would play badminton.

This year was going to be different, very different. I wasn't sure how to handle it.

The younger of my brother's sons and his wife had a new baby and lived on a little farm about an hour and half away. They decided to have Thanksgiving at their house that year, farm-style. It would be great to take Mom down to see them and get her out of the center for the day.

Thanksgiving morning, my husband and I picked up Mom from the center. She looked pretty in her autumn outfit and even had a little make-up and lipstick on. We walked her to the car using her walker. We hated that wheelchair and were always glad to sneak her out of it when we could.

We started our drive down to my nephew's farm. It was a long drive and I began to think, *"Mom may not be able to last very long down at the farm. I'm not sure what time they will actually eat so maybe we should stop on the way and eat somewhere so she won't get hungry?"*

We decided to stop at the Cracker Barrel on the way. This was our first Thanksgiving dinner at Cracker Barrel and it was delicious!

Everyone was happy to see Mom, *Mema* to the grandkids, and they lovingly cared for her during her visit.

Thanksgiving turned out to be pretty good. I was glad that we stopped and ate on the way. As I thought, the trip and visit were a bit much for Mom. Her strength just wasn't what it used to be and she tired quickly. Everyone understood when we decided we needed to leave early and take Mom back to the center.

"Bye bye," Mom said to the kids and grandkids. *"Bye bye."* I think that's all she could think to say.

It was a long ride back to the center and Mom dozed off and on all the way. By the time we pulled up at the center she was tired and weak. We walked her to her room and the nurse came in to check on her.

"How was your day, Mrs. Fleeman?" she asked. *"Did you have a nice Thanksgiving with your family?"*

Mom replied with a nod and said, *"Uh-huh, I'm tired."*

"Well let's get you ready for bed now," said the nurse. My husband and I gave her a kiss and told her we would see her tomorrow. *"I love you, Mom,"* I said as I left. It was a good day.

Before we knew it, Christmas-time was upon us. This Christmas was sure to be different too. The Center was beautifully decorated with huge poinsettias everywhere and red and gold wreaths, bows and ornaments. I decorated her room with a ceramic-lighted Christmas tree that was her mother's and a few other decorations that we'd packed away from Mom's house. In the main lobby there was a grand piano. Once a week before Christmas, the residents in Mom's wing would gather for caroling. I came a few times and would sit and sing with Mom. It was joyful.

The center had a yearly Christmas party for the residents the week before Christmas complete with a *real*

Santa and sacks of gifts for each resident. My brother and I accompanied Mom to the party and stood with her while she sat on Santa's lap for pictures. Santa flirted a bit with her, telling her how pretty she was, which made Mom giddy with pride. The party continued downstairs in one of the banquet rooms. There were tables of holiday food, Christmas cookies, cakes, punch and much more. I fixed her a plate of cookies, fruitcake *(she's the only person in the world that I've ever known that actually liked fruitcake)*, punch and other assorted sweet treats. We sat with her friends and enjoyed the party.

After the party, we took her back to her room and she wanted to go through her *Santa Sack* right away. Several church volunteer groups had gathered the gifts and stuffed the sacks. They were given a list of each resident and tried to fit the gifts to the person. Mom pulled out lotions, sweet smelling body wash, Christmas ornaments, books, calendars, socks, candy and a huge sweatshirt.

"Mom," I said, *"I think that shirt might be too big for you. Maybe I should see if I can swap it out with someone else."*

"No," she said. *"It's mine. It's mine. It was given to me and it's mine. I want to keep it."*

Not wanting to argue I said, *"OK, it's a very pretty shirt. I'll hang it up in the closet for you."*

My brother and I spent all day with Mom for the party and we really needed to get back to work so we could salvage some of the work day.

"OK, Mom," my brother said. *"We need to get back to work. We'll see you later."*

I kissed her and we left. My heart ached every time I left her. In the car, my brother and I talked about how different Christmas would be this year and how we would go about it with Mom. It's tradition for my family to have our Christmas celebration on Christmas Eve. We hosted a huge family party including our immediate family, kids, grandkids, aunt, uncles, and cousins. There would be about 50-60 people all bringing food and presents. It was always chaotic and exhausting. On Christmas morning we always packed up and went to Mom's house for the Fleeman side of the family, which was small - just Mom, my daughter, my brother and his two sons with their wives and kids.

We'd have a big Christmas brunch and then open the gifts Mom so carefully selected for each of us. The gifts were terrible! I don't know who she was shopping for, but rarely did she give us anything that we needed, wanted or even liked. One year she gave my daughter a set of pencils - it was my daughter's first year as a teacher so I guess Mom thought she would need pencils. Really? Mom had more money than all of us but gave the cheapest gifts. It became a running joke among us and the kids.

"Roy," I said. *"What are we gonna do with Mom this Christmas? How are we gonna handle it? You know*

I HAVE to do the Christmas Eve party thing and that'd be too much for Mom. Guess you'll have to take care of her on Christmas Eve," I said with a smirk.

"Na, uh," he said. *"I'm going to my son's house for Christmas Eve."*

"Then I don't know what to do," I said.

"You know," he said, *"she probably won't even know it's Christmas Eve so let's see about just getting her Christmas morning and spending the day with her."*

"You're right," I said. *"We'll plan for that."*

Fortunately, Christmas was on a Sunday that year. My plan was to pick her up for church then bring her back to my house. My brother would come, we would open gifts and then take her back to the center. It seemed like a short amount of time to spend with her and I didn't feel good about it.

I stressed over Christmas with Mom for days. She'd not been back to the house since she fell and broke her hip months earlier. How would she react? Would she want to stay? Beg me to let her stay? Cry? Would she want to go in her room and stay there? How would I explain to her again that she couldn't stay? My heart was hurting at the thought of what could happen.

One day before Christmas, I talked to one of the nurses at the center and shared my concerns.

"Mom hasn't been back to my house for months," I said with tears in my eyes. *"What do I do if she begs to*

stay or wants to go to her room there?" I asked. *"How do I handle it?"*

She could tell I was worried and gave me the best advice.

"I've been asked this a lot," she said. *"This is what I would do. Go to your house, open gifts, visit for a while and then say, 'Mom, let's go look at the Christmas lights or let's go out to eat.' Do something like that and then bring her back here instead of going back to your house again. This will distract her and she should be OK."*

I picked up Mom Christmas morning. The nurse dressed her in a very pretty pair of dark green slacks and her cashmere Christmas sweater. She looked very pretty.

That year our church was in-between pastors and we were honored to have Nelson Price as our interim pastor. He is one of the most renowned and revered pastors I have ever known. Mom was always excited to come to our church because he would make a point of speaking to her. It was nothing unusual for him. He made a point of making everyone feel special. The Christmas service that morning was perfect.

We followed the advice the nurse had given me and after a small bit of Christmas festivities at our house, I said, *"Mom, let's do something different this year and go out to eat."*

She looked at me with a puzzled look. Mom wanted every holiday to be perfect and for my entire adult life she had a way of putting the pressure on me to make it that way, so not having a big Christmas brunch was unusual and probably disappointing to her.

"We thought we would do something completely different and go to the hibachi Japanese restaurant where they cook in front of you. Won't that be fun?" I asked?

I looked at my brother as if asking for some help.

He said, *"Yeah, Mom, the chef cooks right in front of you, does some tricks and even catches an egg in his hat. On the way, I'll take you to see some Christmas lights. There's a house on the way that really does it up."*

It was a stupid thing to say, but of course since he said it, she was willing to go for it.

We drove two cars to the restaurant. He drove Mom and made the detour to see Christmas lights. My husband and followed soon after. We all met at the Japanese restaurant. Just like in the movie *The Christmas Story,* we had Japanese for Christmas dinner. After dinner, I drove Mom back to the Center and my husband rode back home with my brother. I got Mom back to her room. She was tired and looked a little sad. I leaned over to kiss her and I could see her eyes welling up with tears. I tried to keep from doing the same. She said, *"Thank you for my Christmas present."*

I gave her a big beautiful snow globe with a red bird in it. Mom loved watching the red birds at our house. I had it engraved - TO MOM, CHRISTMAS 2016. It was musical and played *Silent Night*. She seemed to like it.

She said, *"It was a good day. I know you tried hard."*

"I love you, Mom," I said. *"I'll see you tomorrow."*

Oh my gosh how my heart was breaking. Christmas was different and would be different from then on. I got to my car, sat in the parking lot and cried all the way home. I was sad and I was exhausted.

Every good and perfect gift is from above,
coming down from the Father of the
heavenly lights, who does not change like
shifting shadows.

(James 1:17, NIV)

13
New Opportunities

2017 - a new year with new opportunities. We'd made it through 2016 and it was quite a year. I was happy to welcome the new year and hopeful it would be better than the last. If I had only known what lay ahead for me in 2017.

Unfortunately, since I had so much going on in 2016 with Mom's broken hip, my daughter's new baby, my terrible *booger* toe illness and all the issues with moving Mom to a long-term care facility, my business took a big hit and business was down. I thought about it and prayed, asking God how I should proceed. I decided I would have to sell my best asset. I'm not only good at print management consulting, but my truest passion is typography. I designed and printed my own self-promo brochure with an emphasis on typography. I made a target list of my vendors, some clients and a few people I knew who were authors. *"Who better to sell my typography skills to than current authors?"* I thought. My intention was to take their drafts, do the layout and typography and then send their books to print. As I put my brochure and cover letter into the dozen or so addressed envelopes, I spread them all out on my desk and prayed over them. *"Dear Lord, thank you for giving me the skill of typography. Thank you for putting it into my heart to reach out to these people and promote my services to them.*

Please let just one of these letters reach a person who could truly use my skill and let it be a blessing to them. In your precious son's name, Jesus Christ, I pray. Amen."

The letters went straight to the post office and I went on with my business, selling printing to my clients, managing their projects, visiting Mom 4 days a week, taking care of my new granddaughter and doing my best to be a good wife to my wonderful husband. Life was busy again but seemed be on a pretty even keel.

It was Spring and almost every day, I would pass by the sign and watch as the beautiful building seemed to be practically complete and ready to open.

TRELLIS HARBOR
Assisted Living and Memory Care
Opening Spring of 2017

"Liz, this is Christine Cobb. If you remember, we met last year and reserved a space for my mother in the Memory Care unit. I'm calling to find out if you have an opening date yet. We are anxious and excited to move Mom to Trellis Harbor."

"Hi, Christine. We are anxious as well. The build-out is almost complete; however, we still have to wait for the state to give us our permit and that could take a while," Liz replied. *"Would you and your brother like to come and do a walk-through? You can even choose the room you want for your mom."*

"Oh, yes, that would be fantastic," I said.

The next day my brother and I arrived at Trellis Harbor and met Liz for the tour. The building was beautiful, inside and out. In the main lobby was a huge arrangement of orchids, Mom's favorite flower. *"A good sign,"* I thought. The decor was fresh and up-to-date with hues of blue and gold, thick white crown molding along the walls and brightly colored paintings everywhere. There was one painting that caught my eye. It was of an orange, gold and black koi fish, just like the ones we had in our pond that Mom loved to sit and watch.

It smelled clean, fresh and new. It was gorgeous. Heck, I would have loved to live there.

Liz took us down to the Memory Care unit. We walked through the locked door. Liz explained that it stayed locked for the safety of the residents in that wing. As we walked in, the dining room was off to the right - tables properly set, complete with linen napkins, water and tea goblets and center flower arrangements. Directly to the left was the activity room. It included a television, mock fireplace, beautifully upholstered chairs with ottomans. The back of the room had floor to ceiling glass windows and sliding doors that opened to the patio, which the residents and guests could use. The patio extended parallel along the side of the entire wing with meticulous landscaping including birdhouses and bubbling garden water fountains. There were several large empty planters which seemed ready to have something planted in them.

"What are these for?" I asked Liz. *"Why are they empty?"*

"These planters will be used as an activity for the residents. We know so many of them like to garden so we're going to allow them to have their own space to plant flowers and vegetables," she answered.

I looked at my brother and said, *"Oh, Mom will LOVE this. I know she's missed being outside and playing in the dirt."*

"Our mother has quite a green thumb. This will be so great for her," I told Liz.

Mom loved to garden and grow all sorts of plants and flowers. She had a little plaque that she kept on the wall at her house:

> *Heavenly Father, Creator of the world, thank You for the quiet beauty of a single flower ... for the soft caress of a fragrant breeze ... for the heart's delight in a brightly painted butterfly. Thank you, Heavenly Father, for all the happy blessings you gave your children when You created gardens.*
>
> *Anonymous*

I love that plaque and keep it now on my dressing table along with a pink ceramic butterfly she made.

We walked back in and down the hall. We picked out the room we wanted for Mom. Room 104, the first room on the left going down the hallway and across from the beauty salon. The room was as nice as any four-star resort hotel room. Mom would have her own space, her own bathroom and shower, vanity and closet. Two big windows looked out to the garden. She could even sit and watch the birds again.

"You see the room is empty. Each resident can bring their own furniture and decorate it as they wish. We encourage them to make it as much like home as possible," Liz explained.

"Wow, this is perfect for Mom," my brother said. *"I can't wait to show it to her. Can we bring her here and show her?"*

"Once we receive our permit, then our memory care director will set up an appointment to assess your mom. If she passes the assessment, then we will set her move-in date," Liz explained.

"Assessment? What do you mean by assessment?" I asked. *"What does it involve? You didn't mention it when we gave you the deposit to hold her space."* I was getting concerned. Here we are, all excited to move Mom and it may not happen if she doesn't pass an assessment. *"We've been telling Mom we were going to move her for months and now there could be a chance that she won't be accepted?"* I exclaimed back to Liz.

"Don't worry. From what you've told me about your mom, I'm sure she will be accepted. The assessment is really to determine her medical needs and her scale of

memory and cognitive challenges," Liz explained. "One thing though, can your mom walk or does she need a wheelchair? We prefer that all of our residents walk, even if it's with a walker."

"Oh," I answered. "She can definitely walk with the help of her walker. The center always wants her to stay in a wheelchair, but she really doesn't need it. She can walk and we prefer to have her walk too."

As we left, my brother looked at me and said, "Well we better prep Mom up for this assessment. Hope she passes."

"Yeah, me too," I said, "But they still don't have their permit so we have some time to work with her."

"OK, get on it. Start working with her. That's your job," my brother said.

"Thanks," I said. "Appreciate that, bro."

I explained the assessment process to Mom. I could tell she was concerned and scared about it.

"What, what if I don't …," she asked.

Mom was having more and more difficulty with her words and it had gotten to where I would finish sentences for her. It started to become a habit for me.

"Pass the assessment," I said.

"Uh-huh," she answered in a shy voice.

I patted her leg and said, "It's OK, Mom. Don't be scared. I'll handle everything and soon you'll be moving to a brand, new place. You'll have your own room, your own

TV, your own bathroom and even your own garden. Don't worry. I'll take care of it."

So I started prepping Mom. I went to the center every single day from then on and made her walk to build her strength, even though the nurses didn't like it. I talked to her about current events and tried to quiz her. I'd ask her questions that I thought might be asked during her assessment:

- *What is your name?*
- *Where did you grow up?*
- *Do you have any brothers or sisters?*
- *Are you married?*
- *Is your husband alive?*
- *How many children do you have?*
- *Who brought you here today?*
- *What hobbies do you have?*

Simple questions would determine her memory status and help them get to know her better. We worked hard every day and every day she would ask me, *"Am I going today?"*

"Soon," I would tell her. *"Very soon, so let's keep working and walking. One more time down the hall?"*

I spent hours with her every day which kept me away from my work more than I should, but I knew it was necessary. I'd just work late at night to catch up on e-mails and orders.

One morning, I checked my e-mail before going to

the center and I was taken by surprise with a particular message.

"Good morning, friend. I received your letter and your brochure in the mail and I think I might have a book project for you. Are you available for a phone call today?"

The message was from Rev. Nelson Price. I was so excited and thrilled that he wanted ME to help HIM. *"I wonder what he has in mind,"* I thought to myself as I typed my answer to him.

"Good morning, Rev. Price. It's so nice to hear from you today," I wrote. *"What would be a convenient time for me to call you?"*

He answered back right away, *"Is 11:00 convenient for you, my friend?"* Nelson Price referred to everyone as *friend* in his messages and letters. Such a gentlemanly thing to do, I thought.

I called him at exactly at 11:00 a.m.

"Hello, Rev. Price. It is so nice to speak to you. How can I help you? Do you have a project in mind already? Are you working on a book at the moment?" I asked.

"Christine, I have a book about Heaven that I have already written. However, it's only as an e-book. I would like to have it printed so it can be used during some of my seminars and sermons on the subject. Would you be willing to help me and what would you charge?" He

asked.

"My goodness, Rev. Price, I would be honored to work with you on this book. Really, it would be my privilege to work with you. I don't even want to charge you for my time and services. I will only charge you for the actual printing of the book. I'm just thrilled that you called me." I answered back.

"Oh my dear, you must charge me. I certainly don't expect you to do all of this work au gratis," he replied.

"Well, we'll talk about that later. Please tell me more about the book. Do you have a raw manuscript that you can send to me?" I asked. "I can use it to get started with the layout."

"I do," he answered. "But I want to make some changes to the content and I really don't like the cover the last publisher chose. I'll e-mail the manuscript to you and we can talk about a new design for the cover."

"That's fine," I answered. "I'm ready to get started."

I hung up the phone and just sat in my big leather desk chair and prayed. "Thank you, Lord. You always provide. And this time, you provided me with the honor of helping to spread your word through the writings of a person who is a true evangelist."

So I got started on Nelson Price's book, *Heaven: Earth's Ultimate Mystery*, now in print form.

Little did I know at the time how meaningful and

impactful this book would become to me and how God brought us together for a purpose yet to come.

May he give you the desire of your heart
and make all your plans succeed.

(Psalm 20:4, NIV)

14
The Move and the Visitors

At last the day came for Mom to move to Trellis Harbor. She passed the assessment with flying colors and was excited to move. My brother and my husband began moving her bedroom furniture from our home into her new room. Her own bed, nightstands, reclining chair, TV, pictures and paintings. I was busy packing her things at Presbyterian Senior Health Center. *"My goodness, how did she accumulate so much stuff in such little time?"* I thought. But I only wanted to make one moving trip so I packed my car full to the roof and packed Mom in there too.

It was a happy day, but with a tinge of sadness. The three ladies whom Mom had become friends with, especially her roommate, were sad to see her go and I felt sad to be leaving them behind. We'd gotten to know each of them so well and their families too. The nurses and caregivers came in one by one to tell Mom goodbye and to wish her well. Everyone was so kind.

By the time we arrived at Trellis Harbor, my husband and brother had the furniture set up. While they unloaded my car, my daughter and I took off to Target and bought brand new bed linens, comforter, pillows, towels, shower curtain, sweet smelling shampoo, soaps and toiletries. We even bought new nightgowns and underwear for her. By the time we finished decorating, her room practically mimicked her room at our house.

I took her wheelchair that we hated so much, folded it up and put that thing in the closet with the hopes of never needing it again, at least for a long time. Mom was just fine using a walker.

Even though her room was directly across from the beauty salon, it wasn't open yet so I helped Mom take a shower and washed and styled her hair. This was when we first met Quinny, her primary caregiver at Trellis Harbor.

She came in and said, *"You know, you don't have to do all that. That's what we're here for. We're happy you're here and please let me know if you need anything at all."*

Mom and I knew right away that we were going to love Quinny. She had a great sense of humor and was sweet and caring. We became friends right away.

No matter how hard things were for Mom and me, I know there are angels all around and Quinny was one of them.

My brother and I were invited to stay and have dinner with Mom that evening in the dining room for her first meal. It was like going to a fine restaurant. Italian was on the menu that night, green salad, lasagna, garlic toast, iced tea and a choice of dessert. Mom chose the chocolate cake, her favorite.

Next to the door of each of the rooms were shadow boxes with a glass door and a lock. The residents were encouraged to put some of their favorite keepsakes in the shadow box. Something that would show their personality through things they loved or hobbies they had. One gentleman had ocean scenes and fishing gear in his shadow box. We knew he loved to fish and loved the ocean. I put some of Mom's Jack Russell dog figurines in her box along with two of her modeling pictures and a photo of her with a horse. Everyone began to refer to her as *Myrna, the Model.* Her modeling pictures were stunning, resembling the style of Audrey Hepburn.

So she was settled into her beautiful new home only four miles from me. What a relief! I stopped by at different times of the day to see how she was doing and most times she would be involved in an exercise class, or a craft-making session. There was always something planned for the residents: movie nights complete with popcorn and soft drinks, or ice cream socials. Mom even began going on outings on the little transport bus. Sightseeing trips through Kennesaw Mountain, usually with a stop at a nearby bakery for cookies. She seemed happy and was doing well. Although her speech and cognitive skills were still declining, she seemed to be more alert and active. I think it was the staff in general and their attention to her that made such a difference to her.

Not long after Mom moved in, I was working at my desk, particularly working on the *Heaven* book for Nelson Price. It was in the early evening and, somehow, Mom had figured out how to use her cell phone. That was a surprise in itself.

I saw MOM show up on my phone. I thought, *"Oh no, something has happened and she's having someone call me."* But no, surprisingly Mom figured out which button on the phone was my number and dialed me. The conversation we had was unusual and hilarious at the same time. When she spoke, it was as if all of her speech came back and she was as lucid as she could be.

"Hello," I answered reluctantly, thinking it must be a nurse or caregiver calling.

"Chrissy," Mom said in a very stern voice. *"There's a man here that is following me. He's making advances to me and I don't like it. I told him I wasn't going to have it! And I told him to leave me alone, I wasn't interested in him."*

I chuckled back to Mom and said, *"What? What man are you talking about? There's only one man living there now Mom and he's very nice. Are you sure he's following you? Are you sure about all of this?"*

"Yes," she firmly replied. *"And I'm not going to have it!"*

"Mom, I don't think he means anything by his actions. Maybe he's just lonely and wants to be your friend."

"No he's not!" she yelled back. *"He wants to get in my pants and I'm not having it! You're so naive, Chrissy.*

You just don't know how men are."

Mom was hopping mad and all I could think of is *Wow*. Where in the world did all this dialogue come from? Just earlier today she couldn't even get words out that made any sense and now she said I was *naive*. Unbelievable.

"Oh, Mom. I'm sure he's not. I'll talk to Quinny about it tomorrow. Just remember that no one can come into your room because it locks as soon as you close the door. Just keep your door closed. I'll see you in the morning," I told her.

As soon as I hung up with her, I could hardly contain myself. This was just too funny. I called my brother to tell him how she'd called me by herself and what she was telling me. We laughed and laughed.

"Well good," he said. *"Maybe she'll get herself a boyfriend up there. You never know. It'll be good for her."*

"Nope, she said 'she wasn't having it' - her exact words," I laughingly replied. *"SHE WASN'T HAVING IT."*

From then on, she would shy away from the man and give him the *stink eye* as only she could do. It was so sad for him. He absolutely wasn't making advances towards her. He was a *wanderer* Quinny told me. He just walked up and down the halls all the time. He wasn't following Mom. My brother befriended him and found out that he really was a very nice man, used to live close by and missed his family. He had Alzheimer's and his wife who was a small sweet lady just couldn't physically handle him and it wasn't safe for him to be at home any longer.

My brother and I continued to visit Mom regularly. She had settled in well at Trellis Harbor and everyone seemed to love *Myrna the Model.*

Stand up in the presence of the aged,
show respect for the elderly and revere
your God. I am the Lord.

(Leviticus 19:32, NIV)

15
Families are Complicated

Early in May, my sister called and said she wanted to come visit Mom. Yes, I have a sister. There are three of us siblings, my brother, my sister and me. I'm the youngest and the one with all the responsibility of taking care of Mom and everyone else.

My sister was always a bit of an outcast. You know there's one in every family. If you don't believe me just take a close look at your own family. She wasn't pretty, or smart, or talented, she was just her own person and Mom always seemed embarrassed of her. She shunned her and neglected the special needs that she had when she was a child. It was a horrible way to treat her and I do believe that Mom contributed to the way my sister acted.

As my sister became an adult, she made some unwise decisions and put herself in some precarious situations. She had a son out of wedlock, which Mom despised and referred to as the *Bastard*. She couldn't keep a job, was on welfare and food stamps and was always involved with people that seemed to take advantage of her. Just more reasons for disappointment and humiliation in Mom's eyes.

My sister lived in South Georgia, and we rarely saw her. If she called, it was to give us bad news about something or to borrow money, which she *always* said she would pay back. Of course she never did. By this time, my sister had colon cancer for about five years. She had part of her colon and rectum removed and had a colostomy bag. She was not doing well. When she called, she told me the cancer had spread to her lymph nodes and the doctors told her she couldn't handle any more chemotherapy or radiation. She was just too weak.

"Chrissy," she said. *"I want to come see Mom. The doctors say I don't have much longer to live and I want to come see Mom."*

Now I'm thinking to myself, *"Is this really true? Not much longer to live?"* My sister had a way of being very dramatic and stretching the truth as far as she could. We never really knew what to believe.

"Can I come and can I stay with you?" she asked. *"My friend will drive me. I'd like to come next weekend."*

Well, what was I supposed to say, *"No?"* Even though my sister was overlooked and undervalued, by our mom, she's still a child of God and He created her to have value in her own way and I do love her. She is a sweet and caring person and has her own set of people close to her home that she cares for and helps.

Although we hadn't seen her in a long time and she'd never been to my house, all I could think of was, *"Great, now I get to take care of another person and how was I going to tell Mom about her visit."* My stress level was going through the roof. It always did whenever I had any dealings with my sister because she had a way of getting on my very last nerve in about a minute.

But I sucked it up and happily replied, *"Of course you can. I'll get the guest room ready for you and your friend. I look forward to seeing you."*

The next day I went to see Mom and told her about my sister's upcoming visit.

"Mom," I said. *"You'll never guess who's coming next weekend to see you. Melinda is coming."*

"Who?" she asked.

"Melinda, your other daughter. She's coming up next weekend," I explained.

"Oh?" she answered in a questioning way.

"Did she really not remember her?" I thought. *"And will she even recognize her?"* It's been a long time since they had seen each other. This was not going to be easy and I prayed that it would go well.

That next Saturday, I waited and waited for her to arrive. All day long ... She had no concept of time and was NEVER on time for anything. So I waited and waited. She called about 11:00 p.m. And said she was coming through town and would be at my house in about an hour. So the stress started, *"Who shows up at midnight?"* I thought. *"How rude and I'm tired."*

When she and her friend arrived, we all sat at the kitchen table. I'd been shopping and bought all the things that I knew she liked, Mountain Dew, cereal, chips, baked goods and lots of other junk food. I offered to fix them something, but she said she just couldn't eat and then began to pull about five prescription pill bottles out of her purse.

"I have to take all of these," she said. *"And especially this one. It's for pain."*

"Shouldn't you eat first?" I asked.

"Oh no, they work better if I don't," she replied.

I found out later that one of the prescriptions was oxycontin which she'd become addicted to.

"OK," I said. *"Well, there are fresh towels and anything else you might need in the guest bathroom. I'm sure you'd like a hot shower after that long trip."*

"No," she said. *"I only take a bath once a week. It's just too much trouble with this colostomy bag."*

Oh, my gosh. That's either gross or lazy, or maybe both. Mom will really love seeing her looking so unkept, smelling of cigarettes and in clothes that looked like they haven't been washed in quite a while.

My plans were to get up early the next morning and take Melinda and her friend to see Mom, visit for a while, go out to lunch and then Melinda could head back home. No need for her to spend two nights at my house. It would be too much for her anyway. Or would it just be too much for me?

But as usual, when it came to any plans with my sister, they didn't go as I wanted. She and her friend didn't wake up until about 11:00 and by the time we got to Trellis Harbor to see Mom it was noon. I had to call ahead to tell the dining room that Mom wouldn't be eating lunch, even though it was getting past the time for her to eat. I knew she'd be getting hungry.

When we got to Trellis Harbor, I took my sister and her friend to the memory care wing and had them sit in the beautiful family room down the hall. Then I went back to get Mom from her room. I needed to take a minute and prepare Mom for what she was about to see. Melinda didn't look anything like she did the last time we saw her. The cancer aged her. She was extremely thin and had lost some of her teeth. I needed Mom to understand this before they saw each other. Of course, to Melinda, Mom would look different too.

I walked slowly down the hall with Mom and when we got close enough, my sister ran to Mom and hugged her for a long time. I could tell by Mom's reaction that she was confused and uncomfortable.

"Who is this woman hugging me?" I'm sure she was thinking. *"She seems familiar and why is she calling me Mom?"*

We sat in the family area and my sister talked and talked, telling Mom all about her cancer and her home and her son. She told her how the cancer had spread, how sick she was and how badly she'd been wanting to see her.

Mom never said a word.

She would look at my sister and then look at me, look back at her and then back at me. It was awkward.

To break up the time, I said, *"Hey, how about I take us all to the Italian restaurant close by? It's been a while since Mom had her favorite pizza."*

Mom perked up at the thought of pizza!

My sister replied, *"That sounds great, but it's hard for me to eat pizza because of my teeth, but I'm sure I can get something else."*

My sister continued to talk all through lunch. She talked and talked. She even tried to flirt with the handsome waiter.

"OMG. Please stop, you're embarrassing us, Melinda," I told her.

All through lunch, Mom never said a word. Not one word.

After lunch, I could tell Mom was tired and had had enough. She turned and said *"Bye"* to Melinda and started to walk back to her room.

I felt sad for my sister and I explained how Mom's mind, memory and physical strength was just different than what she expected.

"I'm sure Mom was glad to see you, Melinda," I said. *"It's just so hard for her to get her words out so sometimes she just doesn't talk. I know she loves you."*

Quinny came to check on Mom and I took my sister and her friend back to my house. I thought they would want to stay another night, but they wanted to drive back home.

After they left, I called my brother and told him about how awkward the visit was and how it tired Mom out.

"Believe me," I said, *"before this year is over, one of them will pass on. I'm not sure which one, but I can just feel it."*

"Aw, come on," he said. *"Neither of them are that bad. You're just over dramatizing, as usual."*

I hung up the phone and prayed a short prayer, *"Lord I know there is healing in your touch and I trust in you. Amen."*

Get rid of all bitterness, rage and anger, brawling and slander, along with every form of malice. Be kind and compassionate to one another, forgiving each other, just as in Christ God forgave you.

(Ephesians 4:31-32, NIV)

16
Second Trip to the ER

It was June 1st. A Thursday. I was getting ready for work and had a busy day working on the first round of edits to the *Heaven* book for Rev. Nelson Price.

My cell phone rang and I recognized the number, Trellis Harbor. *"What a way to start the day,"* I thought. *"I wonder what's the matter."*

"Hello," I said.

"Mrs. Cobb?" asked the person on the other end of the line. *"This is the unit nurse at Trellis Harbor. We're transporting your mother to the emergency room. We've called an ambulance and you should meet her at the hospital."*

"What?" I exclaimed. *"What's wrong, what happened?"*

"We're not sure," she said. *"We checked her early this morning and she had a low-grade fever so we gave her some something for it. We checked her a few minutes later and she was unresponsive."*

"Unresponsive. What do you mean unresponsive?" I asked in terror. *"Was she unconscious?"*

"No," she replied. *"Not unconscious, just unresponsive."*

"What's the difference?" I thought. *"Unresponsive is pretty serious."*

The unit nurse replied, *"She may have some sort of virus or perhaps a UTI which is not uncommon for elderly ladies. We are just erring on the side of caution and sending her to the hospital. I'm sure they'll determine the problem, treat her with some antibiotics and she'll be coming back in no time."*

"OK, thank you," I answered. Then I sped like lightning to the hospital emergency room.

I ran through the doors and frantically asked the check-in nurse, *"Myrna Fleeman? She was sent here by ambulance from Trellis Harbor. I'm her daughter. I need to see her right away. I know she's scared and I need to be with her. Where is she?"*

The check-in nurse looked at her computer and replied, *"I see that she's on her way. The ambulance hasn't arrived yet. You can wait here and you'll see her when the ambulance comes."* I went outside and began pacing the ambulance area desperately looking for the ambulance which was bringing Mom.

The ambulance drove up and the EMTs took Mom out of the vehicle on the gurney. She looked pale and limp, not moving and her eyes were closed. I ran to her.

"Mom, Mom. Are you OK?" I asked as I held her arm. *"Mom. Can you hear me? What's wrong, Mom? Can you open your eyes? It's me, Chrissy. I'm here with you and I'll take care of you."*

Once again, we were back in the ER. Having been

there so many times with Mom, I was beginning to know my way around there pretty well and even recognized some of the doctors and nurses.

The nurse came in and took Mom's vitals. Blood pressure was very high with a slight fever and oxygen level was low. They took vials and vials of blood samples - enough for any vampire to feast upon. And then we waited. Mom seemed to be going in and out of sleep. The ER doctor came in after what seemed like hours and said, *"Mrs. Cobb, we don't see anything significant from your mom's preliminary blood tests, but clearly something is wrong. We'd like to keep her overnight for observation."*

"What do you mean? You can't tell me what's wrong with her?" I exclaimed back to the doctor. *"Does she have the flu or a virus or infection of some sort?"*

"We will continue to monitor her and perhaps something will show in the tests. We're admitting her and sending her up to Room 305 on the Green Level," he replied. *"She'll be given fluids and a general antibiotic and I'm sure she'll be fine in 24 hours or so. The hospitalist physician assigned to her will take it from here."*

"OK, doctor," I reluctantly replied and followed as they wheeled her up to the green level. I'd heard terrible things about the green level of the hospital. It's where the elderly patients were taken and it seemed more like a nursing home than a floor in the hospital. I sat with Mom

and waited for the doctor to come in.

In the meantime, the nurse came in and unhooked her from the bag of fluids and the bag of antibiotics that she was given in the ER. Mom seemed to be coming around by this time and could at least speak to me.

"Mom, do you know where you are?" I *asked.* *"How are you feeling?"*

She looked at me and just said, *"Uh-huh. Tired. Head hurts. Cold."*

We continued to wait for the doctor for hours. No doctor. I kept asking the nurse, *"Where is my mother's doctor? I want to speak to her. It's getting late and she hasn't been seen. What's the plan? I can see that she has not been given any more medication or fluids for hours. I don't understand why she's here and what's wrong with her,"* I pleaded with the nurse. *"I want to speak to her doctor."*

The nurse replied, *"The doctor has gone for the day. She usually makes rounds early in the morning. You can see her then if you're here."*

"OK," I answered. *"But what are her orders? Has more antibiotics or medicine been ordered? Any news from the additional blood tests?"*

The nurse looked at her chart and then back at her computer. *"Hmm, I don't have any orders at all for your mother. So, no, she won't receive any more medication until I hear from the doctor."*

I was dumbfounded and frustrated. Why couldn't anyone tell me why Mom was here, what was wrong with her and what they are going to do to treat her?

I stayed until around 10:00 p.m. when I knew Mom was sleeping soundly. I vowed to be back at 6:00 a.m. to be sure I wouldn't miss the doctor on her morning rounds.

The next morning when I arrived early, Mom was awake. *"Mom, has the doctor come in to see you?"* I asked.

She shook her head as if to say no.

"OK, well, I'm sure she'll be here soon." I said.

And we waited - waited and waited. When the nurse finally came in to take Mom's vitals I asked, *"What's her temperature? She still feels hot to me. Has she been given anything for the fever? Any Tylenol or anything?"*

"Her temperature is 99.9," she replied. *"No fever and no, she hasn't been given any medication. I have nothing on her orders."*

"What?" I exclaimed back to her. *"99.9 IS a fever! I know my mom and her body temperature is always below the normal 98.7. So, YES, she has a fever and needs at least some Tylenol. And what about her daily medications? Her warfarin and blood pressure medicine. Have you given her that?"*

The nurse replied, *"No, we have no orders. I can give her an antacid so she can stomach her breakfast. We give it to all the patients on this floor."*

Now I was angry. *"She doesn't need an antacid,"* I

yelled back to her. *"We need to know what's wrong with her and what treatment she'll receive."* I was fired up angry. *"I demand to see the doctor."*

The doctor, a very highly esteemed physician, finally came in to see my mother, but she brought about 8 med students with her. She never once laid a hand on my mom: didn't listen to her heart, didn't look at her chart, didn't even speak to her. She only spoke to the students. Thank goodness Mom was sleeping and didn't notice. But I sure did. As the doctor and the group turned to leave the room, I followed her out.

"Please tell me what's wrong with my mother. Have you seen anything else in the blood tests? Will she get more antibiotics? She has a fever. Can you at least tell the nurse to give her something for it?"

The doctor flippantly replied, *"I haven't had a chance to review her tests. I'll be back this afternoon."* Then she left. Still no information or even a Tylenol for her fever and body aches.

So I waited for the doctor to come back - waited all day. Mom woke around lunch time and I tried to get her to eat a bite.

"How about a milkshake, Mom? I'll go and get one for you." She shook her head no and just wanted something to drink. So I helped her with some water and tried to get her to eat a bite of a sandwich.

I could tell she felt horrible. She was in pain with

body aches from the fever. She said her head hurt. Then she began to cry. *"I want to go home. I want to go home,"* was all she would say.

I wasn't sure if she meant *home* back to Trellis Harbor, or *home* meaning going to Heaven.

I tried to comfort her. *"Mom, you know I'm working on this book about Heaven with Rev. Nelson Price. Do you want me to read a little to you?"* She didn't answer, so I found an excerpt from the book about angels and began to read:

> *"Angels - They are the ordinary messengers to mankind. In Hebrew, they are called mal'akh, a Persian word meaning courier or messenger. They are more in contact with earthly matters than any other choir. Reference: "He shall give His angels charge over you, to keep you..." (Luke 4:10). Angels are ministering spirits and do not have bodies. Jesus said, "...a spirit does not have flesh and bones" (Luke 24:39). On very special rare occasions certain ones can take on the appearance of a human being. How else could we "entertain angels unaware" (Hebrews 13:2). Their appearance is sometimes radiantly white and blazing with glory (Matthew 28:22) When Bible characters saw angels, they were always adult angels and not chubby infants."[1]*

"See Mom, angels are real. Isn't that good news?" I said to her, choking back tears.

---

[1] Price, Nelson. *Heaven: Earth's Ultimate Mystery.* Self-published 2014. P. 40.

Since we still didn't know what was wrong with Mom, I was scared and so was she. And now I was sad because she just kept crying, *"I want to go home. I want to go home."*

I stayed by her side all day and never left because I wanted to be sure to talk to the doctor. The nurses came in and out and changed shifts. New nurses came in, but still no doctor or medication.

By 4:00 that afternoon, I was absolutely fired up mad. I called for the nurse. *"I demand to see her doctor and if I don't see her doctor within the next 30 minutes, I'm going downstairs to administration and file a complaint. My mother has NOT been treated or seen or even evaluated by a doctor since we've been put in this room. The 30 minutes starts now!"*

The nurse immediately took to her phone and paged the doctor. I saw her speak on the phone for a few minutes but couldn't hear the conversation. Then the nurse came over and said, *"Dr. Williams will not be coming back to the hospital today but would like to speak to you on the phone."*

"OK. Let me speak to her and I want you to stand by me so you can witness my end of the conversation."

"Hello, Dr. Williams," I said. *"I would like some answers. Why have you not examined my mother? Why have you not given any orders to the nurse for any type of medication? She's been in pain and you wouldn't even*

prescribe a simple Tylenol. And she's had no fluids for almost 24 hours now. Even I know that a person with a fever should be treated with fluids. I want to know what's wrong with her and why we are spending yet another night in the hospital."

Dr. Williams answered, "Oh, I have been to see your mother. I came this morning."

"Yes, you came this morning with your students, but you didn't lay one hand on her nor examine her in any way." I shouted back. "You said you would be back to talk to me and you never came back. I haven't left her side so I know you've not been in to see her."

I could hear the doctor typing on her computer through the phone as if she were trying to find information on Mom.

"I want to know what resulted from the blood tests. I want to know why she hasn't been given any treatment for over 24 hours. Can you tell me that please?" I was steaming at this point because I knew the doctor didn't have a clue about my mother.

"Actually, Dr. Williams, it is my impression that you completely forgot about my mother - YOUR patient!" I yelled into the phone.

Dr. Williams calmly replied, "Please give the phone back to the nurse. I will see you and your mother in the morning."

After that phone call, several nurses hurried into

the room and Mom was given fluids, Tylenol and an antibiotic again. This goes to show you that you shouldn't always rely on the doctors and nurses. As a family member or caregiver or even a patient, sometimes you have to take matters into your own hands and make some demands.

I later apologized to the nurse. *"I know none of this is your fault and I'm not upset with you. Your hands were tied until you could receive orders from the doctor. I understand that and I know you tried to contact her many times. It's unfortunate that I had to threaten to go to management in order to get the doctor's attention. I really do believe she forgot about my mother."*

"Yes ma'am," she answered.

I wasn't sure if she was agreeing to what I said about the doctor or just acknowledging my apology. I think she knew the doctor was non-attentive to Mom.

The next morning, Dr. Williams finally showed up to examine Mom. She listened to her heart and had her breathe in and out and that was all she did. Then she told me she was changing Mom's regimen of medicine. She wanted her to take organic medicine.

"What?" I thought to myself. *"Is this doctor just crazy or stupid? Why would she take her off her Warfarin and blood pressure medicine that she'd been taking for years?"*

Dr. Williams said, *"She's fine and I don't have a diagnosis or anything so I am going to discharge her."*

"OK, so we've been here going on three days and you have no idea of what could have caused her to feel so bad? Is that what you're telling me?" I questioned.

"Yes, she's fine," replied Dr. Williams.

Oh, my wheels had been turning and I already had a list of notes about this hospital visit and Dr. Williams. The hospital would hear from me and you could count on that.

I called the head of the memory care unit at Trellis Harbor and told her that Mom was being discharged. I wasn't sure if they would allow her to come back since the hospital didn't diagnose her with any particular illness.

She asked, *"What's her diagnosis? Is she contagious?"*

She then informed me that since Mom was ill and was hospitalized that she would need 24-hour supervision for 7 days when she returns and referred me to a sitting service.

I stayed with her through the first night until the first sitter came the next morning. She was a lovely lady and Mom immediately took to her. Of course, Mom felt like she was *Queen for a Week*, by having a personal sitter every day.

I will say that the daily one-on-one attention did seem to help Mom quite a bit. She seemed happier. By the end of the week, with the help of the sitters making her walk, she seemed stronger too. If she was happy, I was happy.

The righteous cry out, and the Lord hears them; he delivers them from all their troubles.

(Psalm 34:17, NIV)

17
Who is Myrna?

It's time you met my Mom.

Myrna grew up in Miami, Florida. She was the only child of her parents. Her mother worked for Western Union and her father was a banker, on the board of several banking institutions throughout his career. During her early years she enjoyed ballet, golf outings with her father, fun on the beautiful Miami beaches and summer trips to Highlands, NC, where she first found her love of horses. She attended Miami High School where she was a majorette. After high school, Myrna began her modeling career. She worked as model for print photos and runway fashion with the Coronet Modeling Agency. Her favorite modeling shoot was on the beach, when she wore a gold lamé bathing suit. Myrna was beautiful then and beautiful always.

She married my dad in 1956. Her beautiful and elaborate wedding was considered a *high society* social event at that time in Miami. She even modeled her wedding dress and the photos were used in wedding magazines.

During her marriage and while living in Miami, she had two children, my brother and my sister. Her husband was a horse trainer. Myrna loved the opportunity to be involved with the horses. After living in Miami for some time, Dad was offered a job as a horse trainer for a new stable. The family moved to New Jersey, where I was born. It was hard to conform to the cold winters of the north for these *sun birds* of Miami so they moved back down south to Tampa. My dad became the trainer for the Tampa Yacht Club Stables. Mom enjoyed a wonderful social life there and began to show the American Saddlebred Horses that Dad trained.

In 1969 we moved again and settled nicely in Marietta, Georgia. Mom and Dad divorced many years later and Mom began a career as a riding instructor. She loved being around the horses and, even more so, loved to see her students enjoying them as well. Her focus was Saddle Seat Equitation and she sent a few riders on to become champions in show.

Myrna moved her riding instruction business to Henderson Stables in College Park, Georgia, run by Dewey Henderson. Myrna and Dewey became a great team and continued the horse show circuit for many years. As sometimes happens in partnerships, they fell in love and became a pair. He was undoubtedly the love of Mom's life.

In 1978 they decided to move away from horse training and teaching. Myrna helped Dewey with his aspiration to build a horse auction facility that became a highly recognized auction and event venue in Union City, Georgia - Henderson Auction Arena. In keeping with her love of horses and riding students, she opened her own shop within the facility, the Hobby Horse Tack Shop. During this time, Mom and Dewey became synonymous with each other and were widely known throughout the horse industry. They also became active in business and social events in South Fulton County where the auction facility was located.

Sadly, Dewey succumbed to cancer in 1987. Mom was heartbroken. Soon after his death, Henderson Auction Arena was sold. She took some time to contemplate her life and decided to try her hand at real estate. This is where her career really took off. She started small by selling houses with Fuller Real Estate Company. She excelled in her real estate career and became even more well known in the South Fulton area. She was elected president of the South Fulton Chamber of Commerce in 1991. She was a member of the American Cancer Society as well. Soon she tired of selling houses and turned her attention to commercial real estate with Metro Brokers. During this time, she built a new home in Fayetteville, Georgia. She worked as a premier real estate agent until she retired at the age of 72.

Myrna was active in the Fairburn community. The United Methodist church in town was her church home where she taught Sunday School for many years. She served on several committees and helped organize church social events. She was a volunteer at Cochran Mill Nature Park. She loved the nature center and enjoyed teaching others about the animals and natural foliage. Myrna was a part of the *Knit Whits* – a group that knitted shawls and donated to other organizations to distribute to people who were ill. She started a book club with friends and developed a nice library in her home. Myrna enjoyed the classics such as the Atlanta Symphony Orchestra, the theater and the opera. There was always beautiful music playing in her home. She loved the outdoors and gardening. She especially had a gift with orchids. Friends would bring their dying orchid plants to her and she had a way of bringing them back to life. She was a *dog person* too and doted on her precious Jack Russell Terriers. They were her comfort and her companions.

No matter what organization or person Myrna was with, she always left a lasting impression of kindness, professionalism, and a wealth of knowledge.

. . .Yup, she left a lasting impression alright.

Live in harmony with one another. Do not be proud, but be willing to associate with people of low position. Do not be conceited. Do not repay anyone evil for evil. Be careful to do what is right in the eyes of everyone.

(Romans 12:16, NIV)

18
It Happened

I remember July 28th, a Friday. I'd put off having surgery to repair my *booger* toe until this day, thinking I would have the weekend to stay off my feet. Surgery was scheduled for 1:00 p.m. I woke up early that day so I could go see Mom before I went to the hospital. I needed to let her know about the surgery and that I wouldn't be able to come to see her again for a few days. She was doing great back at Trellis Harbor so I thought taking off a few days for the surgery was perfect timing.

I showered that morning. It was a no make-up day due to the instructions for surgery so I dressed in my most comfortable long, jersey skirt and black T-shirt with a white sweater. Even though it was the middle of summer in Georgia, I still always took a light sweater. I put on my favorite black sandals and I was ready to go ... so I thought.

At about 8:00 a.m. I received a call from Trellis Harbor. This time it was Shelly, the head of the memory care unit.

"Christine?" she asked.

"Yes. Hi Shelly. I was just about to leave to come see Mom. Is everything OK?" I asked.

"Well, no, not at all," she said. *"Your mom fell this morning and hit her head. We've called the EMTs and they are on their way to the ER with her. You really need*

to go there as quickly as possible."

"Oh no!" I exclaimed. *"I'll leave right now. Thank you for calling and I'll let you know what the doctors say once I get there."*

"Yes, please call me and let me know. Everyone is concerned about her," she said.

I rushed to grab my purse and keys and took off driving like a bat out of hell to the hospital ER, once again. As I was driving, I was selfishly thinking to myself, *"Well, this is just like Mom to pull something like this on the very day I had surgery scheduled. I'm sure she just has a bump on the head. They'll do some CT scans and send her back to Trellis Harbor. But I should call my doctor and reschedule the surgery. The anesthesiologist, the surgeon, the operating room, everything and everyone was planning for the surgery. Ugh, this will be a hard call to make, but I have no choice. I need to stay with Mom. I sure hope I don't have to pay for all of their wasted time."*

This time as I arrived at the ER, I met the EMTs as they were wheeling Mom in.

"Are you her daughter?" one of them asked. *"Shelly from Trellis Harbor told us to be sure to speak to you when we arrive."*

"Yes, yes. *I'm her daughter,"* I answered as I was trying to keep up with them. They were in much more of a hurry than any other time she'd been taken to the hospital.

I could feel their urgency to get her to the examining room quickly. The doctor and nurses had been notified by the EMTs and they were ready for Mom. Now I was getting scared. This was different, very different.

"What's going on? What's wrong with her? How bad is it. Just a bump on the head, right? Please tell me," I anxiously asked the EMT.

"Ma'am," he said. *"She hit her head pretty hard and there's already a swollen area the size of a golf ball. The doctor will examine her and tell you more."*

The nurses quickly hooked Mom up to some IV's as they always do when anyone is admitted to the ER. The doctor examined her quickly and shouted, *"CT scan, STAT!"* And they whisked Mom away.

The doctor looked at me and said, *"I'll know more very soon, but if you have any plans for today, you'd better cancel them."*

"This is bad. This sounds real bad," I thought to myself. *"I'd better call my brother. I need to call my husband too."*

While she was out of the room for the CT scan I called my brother, Roy. Roy had just started a new job and I knew he was probably far from the hospital.

"Roy?" I said in a voice that I'm sure sounded anxious.

"Yeah. What's up?" he answered.

"It's Mom, Roy. She's at the ER. She's out for a CT

scan now, but the doctor already told me to cancel everything for this afternoon. Roy this is serious. I need you to come, please," I explained.

"How bad is it?" he asked.

"I don't know yet, but the doctor told me to stay close and he would be back soon to tell me what's going on. All I know is that she fell and hit her head at Trellis Harbor," I answered. "Please hurry."

"OK. Let me call my boss and let him know," Roy said. "I'll be there as quickly as possible."

Then I called my husband and told him the same thing. Without any hesitation, he said, "I'll be right there."

About this time the doctor returned and told me the news.

"Your mom has a large hematoma and from the CT scan there is bleeding in her brain and around the skull. Her brain is swelling. We're sending her up to the Neurology ICU. The neurologist on call up there will take it from here. You can follow her up there."

I immediately called Roy back. "The doctor said Mom has bleeding on the brain and her brain is swelling. We're going up to the Neurology ICU. You need to hurry."

"OK," he said. I think he was in such shock that he just couldn't say anything else.

The nurses in the ICU met us at the door and hurried us into a room. They hooked Mom up to the heart monitor, blood pressure monitor and put an oxygen mask on her to help her breathe.

"Mom, Mom, can you hear me?" I frantically tried to talk to her in hopes that she would give me some sign.

The nurse told me they had given her some morphine for the pain so she may not answer me, but to still try to talk to her. My husband arrived and could immediately see the seriousness of the situation.

There were no words exchanged between us. He just stopped me from pacing, grabbed me and held me as tight as he could. And that's when the tears started. I was so scared.

Roy arrived just a few minutes later.

"What have the doctors told you so far, Chrissy?" he asked me.

"Mom has bleeding within her skull and brain and her brain is swelling. The doctor left to review the CT scan and consult with the surgeon. They may be able to do surgery and relieve the pressure. He should be back pretty soon to talk to us. I'm glad you're here," I told him.

So we waited and watched and continued to try to talk to Mom even though she seemed unconscious.

And we prayed. *"Lord you are merciful and mighty. I know you can help Mom. Please Lord. Please."* It was more begging than praying, I think.

The neurologist came back in the room. My brother introduced himself to him. *"Doc, I'm Roy, her son. Please tell me what you think. What can be done for Mom?"*

The neurologist asked Roy and me to sit down.

"Let's talk for a moment and let me try to explain," he said. *"The scans show that your mom has significant bleeding in the brain and between the brain and the skull. Her brain has already swelled and will continue to swell. This is extremely painful so we're keeping her sedated. I've consulted with the surgeon and we don't feel that she is a candidate for surgery. She will most likely not survive it."*

He stood up and walked over to Mom. He said, *"You see, she is already paralyzed on her left side."*

Then he sat back down by us.

"So what now?" I asked. *"What will happen if she doesn't have surgery?"* I was hoping I wasn't going to hear what I was afraid of hearing. I wanted his answer, but I already knew what he was going to say.

"There's nothing more we can do except help her with the pain," he answered. *"She will die and usually with situations like this and with her injury, I suspect you have about 24 to 48 hours. We're going to move her to another room and I've called the hospital care team and they are going to contact the hospice here behind the hospital to see if there's a room available. You should probably call any other family members or friends. I'm sorry,"* he said. *"I know this is hard and it's one of the hardest things I have to do as a doctor."* And he left the room.

All I can remember is pulling my glasses off, throwing them on the chair and Roy and I held each other and cried. I haven't seen him cry like that since his best friend, Cappy, died.

The whole scenario of what had just taken place beginning with the ER, the neurologist and with my brother constantly replays itself in my mind, even now, like a broken film strip.

Roy left the room and called his two sons to tell them the news. I'd already called my daughter and my sister. While he was gone, I couldn't stop the tears and I just laid my head against Mom.

A nurse came in. *"Honey, what's wrong?"* she said. And then she took a step back and looked at me. I think she knew at that point that Mom was dying. *"I know you from somewhere. You look so familiar. What's your name?"* she asked.

I answered through the tears, *"Christine Cobb."*

"Is this your mother?" she asked. *"What's her name?"*

"Myrna Fleeman," I answered.

"This Miss Myrna?" she exclaimed. *"Miss Myrna? She was at Presbyterian Senior Health Center, wasn't she? I'm Ethel. I used to take care of her on the weekends there. Do you remember me?"*

Not even waiting for my answer she said, *"Oh, honey, I'm so sorry."* Then she hugged me like a mama bear would hug her scared baby cub.

"I will pray for you and for her and your whole family, sweetie," she said as she left the room.

In the following days I came back to the ICU area and looked for Ethel. I even asked other nurses where I might find her. Surprisingly, no one knew Ethel and told me there hasn't been a nurse in that unit named Ethel. I think God sent her there for me at that moment by Mom's bedside. It was He who was hugging me.

It was late that night when Mom was moved out of the ICU room and into a regular hospital room down the hall. She was taken off all monitors and oxygen. Only the IV line was left to administer the morphine. In the morning, we were to be notified of an availability at the hospice center.

"Roy, I'll stay with Mom tonight. You can go home and shower and rest. When you come back in the morning, I'll go home and do the same. Go ahead and go. I'll be fine. Just try to come back early in the morning," I told him.

He stood up, kissed Mom on her forehead and started down to the parking garage.

I was resting in the chair next to Mom and all of the sudden she sat straight up in the hospital bed and started calling out, *"Momma, Momma. Help me Momma. Momma, Momma."* She was pulling at the sheets and seemed as if she was reaching for something or someone.

It scared me to death. Since she had referred to me as her mother many times, I wasn't sure if she was calling for me or her actual mother.

"*Myrna, Myrna,*" I said, calling her by her name, thinking it might get her attention. "*It's OK, I'm right here with you.*"

"*Nurse, nurse, please come quickly,*" I shouted down the hall hoping someone at the nurse's station would hear me.

A nurse came running in. "*What's going on?*" she asked.

"*I don't know. She just sat up and started calling out and acting like she was speaking to someone,*" I answered. "*I thought she was unconscious or sleeping. Why is this happening? What can we do? Is she in pain? She seems like she is in pain,*" I exclaimed. "*Does this mean she is going to be OK?*"

The nurse answered back, "*It's OK. The morphine and the swelling in the brain is causing agitation and hallucinations. I'll request some Ativan to calm her.*"

This episode scared me to death. I could hardly hold Mom down as she was seemingly trying to reach out to someone.

I found my cell phone and called Roy. "*Roy, you need to come back, right away. I can't handle this. Mom is hallucinating. I need your help.*"

He didn't even wait for me to explain before saying,

"I'll be right there. I'm still in the parking garage. Hold on."

He came back and I was so glad. The Ativan was starting to take affect and Mom was back to a sleep-like state. We both stayed the night, taking turns sleeping. The next morning, Roy left very early to go home to shower and change. When he returned, I left and did the same. I rushed as fast as I could so I could get back to Mom.

Around noon, the nurse came in and informed us that Mom would be taken to the hospice and I needed to go ahead to fill out the paperwork. Roy stayed behind and followed the ambulance that transported Mom.

I got in my car and just sat there for a moment. I prayed, *"Lord, I know you are a merciful and loving God. I'm scared, Lord, I'm so scared. I need your strength to get me through this."*

*For I am the Lord your God who takes
hold of your right hand and says to you,
Do not fear; I will help you. Do not be
afraid, you worm Jacob, little Israel, do
not fear, for I myself will help you,"
declares the Lord, your Redeemer, the Holy
One of Israel.*

(Isaiah 41:13-14, NIV)

19
Wasted Prayers

I arrived at the hospice, met the administrator who was waiting for me and filled out all the paperwork. This time, I actually was signing my mom away to death. It seemed so surreal and overwhelming. The chaplain came in to talk to me, the head nurse came to explain the process and the hospice doctor came in as well.

"Mrs. Cobb," the doctor said. *"With this type of injury and swelling on the brain and the brain stem, you may only have about 24 to 48 hours. You should start thinking about making plans, contact your funeral home of choice and begin making those decisions."*

I sat still, in front of all of them, in shock and disbelief. It was if they were talking but I couldn't hear them. I was already exhausted, scared, completely emotional and had an overwhelming feeling of loss. Loss of control and loss of my mom.

My husband, brother and I called the funeral director, who happened to be a friend. I told him that death was imminent and shouldn't be long. He asked a few questions, burial or cremation, church service or the use of their chapel and more questions. I answered as best I could. He finished the call by telling us to call him back as things progressed then come by to discuss the obituary, arrangements, pick out the urn, flowers, reception, etc. I could only think with bewilderment, *"I'm not ready for all of this."*

The hospice nurses are truly caring and compassionate. They are a gift from God and all of them were extraordinary. When I went back into Mom's room, they had her settled comfortably in the bed. I walked over to Mom held her hand and stroked her hair. She looked so peaceful.

The nurse said, *"Sweetie, it may seem like she's asleep or even unconscious because her eyes are closed, but she can still hear your voice. So be sure to talk to her. You may be surprised that she responds to you in some way. And don't be alarmed if you notice a grimace on her face or painful expressions. She's on very strong pain medication and sedation and it's not unusual for this to happen. Please let me know if you have any questions or if I can do anything for you."*

The hospice was a beautiful place and her room was large, with a pull-out sofa and a recliner. There was also a screened porch with rocking chairs which was a wonderful reprieve for us to take quick breaks from Mom's bedside.

I spent the first night on the pull-out sofa, sleeping very little and, of course, thinking that she could go at any minute from the timeline the doctors mentioned.

The next day our pastor came to visit and to pray with us. Our very best friends from church came to visit and to pray. One by one the grandchildren came, my daughter and Roy's two sons. Even some of the ladies from Trellis Harbor came to visit.

By this time we'd surpassed the 48-hour point and there was no change in Mom. I stayed with her day and night for about five days, just going home briefly each day to shower and change. The nurses and my husband finally encouraged me to go home at night and try to get a good night's sleep - then come back the next day. Roy, still new in his job, tried to keep up with his work and come by the hospice every day too.

The days continued as Mom's body slowly shut down. It was about the eighth day, I'd gone home to start gathering photos so I could work on the funeral montage when I got a call from my brother.

"Chrissy, you're not going to believe this, but Mom is awake and she's eating," my brother said.

"What?" I exclaimed in shock. *"Eating? She's awake? Maybe she's actually going to be OK. Maybe the doctors are wrong? Oh, Roy, what have we done?"*

Thankfully, my husband happened to be home at this time because I ran into the house and fell into his arms sobbing, with a wail that I'd never heard come from my body before.

"Oh my gosh," I cried. *"We've been starving her, killing her all these days and she's going to be OK! But then what? She'll have brain damage and it will be even worse. Oh, Lord, what have we done?"* I felt as if I was losing

control of my mind and body.

I rushed back to the hospice to see for myself. The doctor and nurses came in to check on her and on me.

"Doctor, is this normal?" I asked.

"There is no 'normal' in the dying process," he answered. *"It's not uncommon for there to be a rise almost like a rally before death. Believe me, you've not starved her and you aren't killing her. You are humanely allowing her to die peacefully and without pain. The swelling in her brain is extremely painful and at this point irreparable."*

From that point on, I stayed by her side. She slipped back into unconsciousness. And no, she really didn't eat or digest any food, it only seemed that way to my brother. I would stroke her hair and play beautiful piano hymns from my iPhone for her.

I would sing this song to her:

> *Love Remains ...*
> *... And they share joy*
> *And they share pain*
> *But through it all,*
> *love remains.*
> *Kingdoms come and go,*
> *but they don't last*
> *Before you know*
> *the future is the past*
> *In spite of what's been lost*
> *or what's been gained*
> *We're living proof that*
> *love remains.*

... We all live
And we all die
But the end is not goodbye
The sun comes up
And the seasons change
And through it all,
love remains . . .

(Songwriters: Tom Douglas / Jim Daddario)

I wouldn't leave. I kept the *Heaven* book that I was working on with Rev. Nelson Price with me constantly. I would read small passages and then reflect on the scriptures he referred to throughout the book. It was a comfort to me and it was clear to me that God planned for me to work on this particular book. He knew what was going to happen with Mom and He knew this book would be a repose for me.

During this time, one morning, I was honored with a visit from my friend, Nelson Price. We sat out on the porch in the rocking chairs and talked. Then, as he was saying his goodbye, he came in the room and we prayed over Mom. I began to cry, *"Rev. Price,"* I said. *"Sometimes I sit here and ask God to please go ahead and take her home to be with Him. And then other times I ask God to please just give me one more day so I can just look at her."*

And with the most profound words I have ever heard and will always remember, he said, *"My dear, I hear that from so many people that are in this same situation. My friend, those are <u>wasted</u> prayers. God will only take* *her in His time and nothing you can do or say will change that. He created her and only He knows when He will take her to be with Him. If you want to pray, pray for the nurses, pray for your family and give thanks to God for loaning her to you for the time she was on this earth. My dear, pray for God's will to be done."*

Sometimes it takes hearing this from another person, but he was right, as he always was.

I continued to stay with her, night and day. On the morning of the eleventh day, a Sunday, the weekend nurse came in. She was sweet and kind in the way she handled Mom and asked me if I would mind if she prayed. She washed Mom's feet and silently prayed as she did it. She said, *"It won't be much longer, her skin is mottling and her feet are starting to turn purple."*

"Thank you," I said. *"You're an angel."*

I was exhausted and it was still early so I laid back down on the sofa bed only to wake a few minutes later when my best friend I'd grown up with, who knew me better than anyone and who I'd been talking to every day on the phone, came in. We'd not been able to see each other during this time because she herself was taking care of a friend who was dying. Donna was selfless and brought this friend into her home and arranged for home hospice care. The friend died just the day before. As soon as I saw her, I felt a sense of relief. We ran to each other and both cried. She for her friend and me for Mom and pure caring for each other. She couldn't stay long as she had to make arrangements for her friend. After she left it was like the gates opened and people just kept coming to visit.

As I sat and talked with Quinny and Holly, who came to visit from Trellis Harbor, my life story with Mom just started to flow from me without any filter. It was a shock to both of them.

"You know," I said. *"She was a terrible mother."* They both looked at me as if I had just grown devil horns.

"What?" Quinny said. *"You've always acted like you were so close to her. Ya'll visited her more often than any other family member of a resident I've ever known and you care for her with such love."* She shook her head, *"Girl, you gotta explain this one to me."*

"Well, yes, I do take good care of her and I do love her because she's my mom," I answered. *"The responsibility is mine. Who else would take care of her? Besides that, I'm a Christian and it is written: 'Honor your father and your mother, as the Lord your God has commanded you ...'"* (Deuteronomy 5:16, NIV).

"Go on," Quinny said.

"OK, I'll try to sum it up for you." And I started to explain, *"So my mom and dad divorced when I was eleven. She threw him out because he was a full-blown alcoholic. Then she fell in love with another man. That love must have been pretty strong because she left us for him. Yup, you heard me right. She left us. She'd leave for*

days at a time and we took care of ourselves. She'd give us money for groceries, but she wasn't there to cook or have meals with us. Heck, she didn't even know if we were going to school or playing hooky. Mom's priorities were always herself first, her love second, her money third, her notoriety fourth and her kids last. For instance, when I was in high school, I was in a Valentine Pageant - - Mom didn't come. I thought Mom would be so proud of me. It was an important event for me because I was chosen by my classmates to be one of the contestants."

"One year on my birthday she said she was out of town with her man, so my birthday was blown off as usual. Then I got a call from her asking me to meet her at the local hotel where they were 'having some alone time' for the weekend so we could have birthday cake. She had lots of money, but always had an excuse not to spend it on her kids. No help with cars or college and certainly little money spent on weddings for any of us. And most of all, she was very judgmental, not only to us, but to other people too. She was very critical if I gained a little weight and especially if Roy gained any. She had no problem letting us know that she 'noticed a little extra weight' on either of us. She had four grandchildren whom she very rarely spent time with. Never came to any of their special events either. And when I married Ty, he had two daughters from his first marriage, which then became my stepdaughters and are a very important part of my life.

Mom would have nothing to do with them and didn't agree that they were part of her family."

"Mom very rarely said 'I love you' or 'I'm proud of you.' She was not affectionate at all. I know a lot of people had it much worse with their parents, but when I became a mom, it hit me like a ton of bricks – Mom was never there for us and I was going to make damn sure that my kids knew they were number one to me, no matter what."

The Apostle Peter said:

> Be shepherds of God's flock that is under your care, watching over them—not because you must, but because you are willing, as God wants you to be; not pursuing dishonest gain, but eager to serve; not lording it over those entrusted to you, but being examples to the flock. (1 Peter 5:2-3, NIV)

I continued to explain, "Even though she was a bad mom, I still love her and I always admired her beauty and sense of style and charisma. Look at her now, here on her death bed. She's still beautiful and I will honor her always, because it's God's commandment to do so." Then I realized this was probably her last day on earth and oh what she has missed.

Holly, sitting quietly listening to me, said, "Christine, I have to tell you something. One day when I was walking with your mom in the courtyard at Trellis

Harbor, she asked me to sit down – she wanted to talk. It was almost like she was making a confession. In her words, speaking as best as she could, she said she knew she was not a good mother and she regretted it immensely."

"I know," I replied to Holly. "I do believe that. It's so sad that she didn't have the time to say it to us. But it is what it is and I don't have any bitterness about it. I appreciate you telling me about your conversation with her though. It means a lot."

It was starting to get late and I was completely exhausted. My husband came back into the room and Holly and Quinny said their good-byes.

I sat back down on the pull-out sofa bed and felt totally spent of any energy and all emotion. I felt like it was her last day and I wanted to stay with her. Around 10:00 p.m. my husband, along with one of the nurses, encouraged me to go home and get some rest.

The nurse explained, "You know, I've heard that if the dying person senses you are close by, they resist dying because they know the pain it will cause you. I've seen instances when a spouse or child will leave for a cup of coffee and come back and their loved one has passed while they were gone. I promise you when her heartbeat begins to slow down, I'll call you right away."

"OK," I answered. "You may be right. I only live about ten minutes from here so please promise to call me."

When I got home, I laid out my clothes so I could slip

into them quickly when the nurse called and got into bed.

At 5:00 a.m. The next morning, July 10th, 2017, the nurse called.

"Ms. Cobb," she said. *"Your mother's heart has slowed and I don't think it will be long now. Please hurry so you can be with her."*

When we arrived about 15 minutes after the call from the nurse, Mom had just passed. I went in the room anyway and kissed her forehead.

"I love you, Mom." I said. *"I will see you again one day. And you <u>were</u> a good mom."*

Love is patient, love is kind. It does not envy, it does not boast, it is not proud. It does not dishonor others, it is not self-seeking, it is not easily angered, it keeps no record of wrongs. Love does not delight in evil but rejoices with the truth.

(1 Corinthians 13: 4-6, NIV)

Epilogue

God always has a plan and he lays that path out before us. He knows what we need and exactly when we'll need it. There were so many events that happened through this time and, through my faith in Him, I know it was He who provided.

He gave me my brother back and He came into his life, pushing out the alcoholism.

By leaving little dimes, my hints from Him, I was reminded to always put others first and that God is always with me.

He put people in my life along this journey that He knew would be of help and importance to me. He sent our church the perfect pastor through Mom's stay at Presbyterian Senior Health Center. And by this more people have come to know Him.

Having the opportunity to work on the Heaven book with Rev. Nelson Price was a perfect example of God's perfect timing. The book meant so much to me and I needed to be reminded of God's everlasting love and that our time here on earth is only for a short time. Our eternal life is with Him.

For it is by grace you have been saved, through faith—and this is not from yourselves, it is the gift of God— not by works, so that no one can boast. For we are God's handiwork, created in Christ Jesus to do good works, which God prepared in advance for us to do.

(Ephesians 2:8-10, NIV)

Always keep your eyes and heart open. You just might find a dime in the sand.

About the Author

Christine Cobb lives in Marietta, Georgia. She rode and showed American Saddlebred horses during her childhood and teen years. Her love for horses is unending and on the back of a horse is where she finds her happiness. She is active in her  church, as part of the Mission Team and Founder of PEARLS, Women's Ministry.

She started her career in the graphics industry at a Fortune 500 company. This is where Christine learned not only to strive for, but to achieve and maintain the highest level of performance, perfection, and the significance of hard work. She took on the mantra of *"It's not what you say, it's what you do that matters, so do it well."* This mindset has brought her to where she is today, successful in the printing business and providing quality professional services to her clients every day. You can find Christine on LinkedIn at: <u>LinkedIn.com/in/ChristineCobb</u>

Christine took a solo trip to a ranch in Montana on the one-year anniversary of her mother's death. Amid the fresh air, fields of lavender, and hundreds of horses, she began writing this book.

She enjoys traveling her husband, Ty, and spending time with her children, grandchildren, friends, and her beloved dalmatian, *Maizy*.

More great resources from WordTruth Press

Heaven
Your Amazing Journey Home

Jesus gave you this amazing promise:
In my Father's house are
many rooms. I go there
to prepare a place for you.

What an amazing grace indeed is this place He calls Heaven. And Jesus wants you to be with Him there — He wants you to make the journey home.

Heaven reveals both the present hope and incredible future for all who believe.

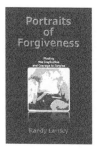

Portraits of Forgiveness (2nd. Ed.)
Finding the Inspiration and
Courage to Forgive

Like an old, frayed blanket there are many loose threads in our relationships. Issues and conflict divide us from family, friends, and innumerable people we encounter throughout life. The process of forgiveness is necessary to restore and rebuild those relationships. In this book you will find great stories of how God works in the lives of people to bring about forgiveness and reconciliation - binding up the loose threads and making relationships even stronger than before. Includes small group study guide and teacher's guide.

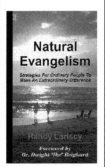	**Natural Evangelism** *Strategies for Ordinary People to Make an Extraordinary Difference* Evangelism should be as natural as breathing but for many believers it is a word that leaves you breathless. Natural Evangelism is a lifestyle of sharing the love and message of Christ in the context of relationships you form along the way. Discover five long-term strategies that ordinary believers can practice in their everyday life zones. Use these strategies to develop prospects, create natural opportunities to share the good news, and see people develop a personal relationship with the LORD Jesus.
	The Ten Commandments *Evangelism Tract (Qty 50)* The Ten Commandments are shown on the front of this 3x5 card with a positive version of each command. On the back is a presentation of the gospel. It is printed with a glossy, color front and black-and-white back.
	**The Good News of GRACE** *Evangelism Tract (Qty 50)* This attractive 3x5 card presents the good news using the word GRACE as an acrostic. Each letter represents a different aspect of God's grace at work in salvation. Glossy, color front and black-and-white back.

	### Speedy Devotions *Volume One – Wise Choices* Do you have only a little time to study the Bible? Or does the Bible seem intimidating in its size and scope? Many find it hard to stay focused on long passages of Scripture. Yet the Bible is God's word for all people. And even a small amount of God's word can have a profound impact on your life. Volume 1 is about wise choices. This devotional takes you through the book of Proverbs where you learn great wisdom in small portions each day
 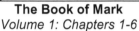	### The Book of Mark *Volume 1: Chapters 1-6* The Insight Bible Commentary Series (IBC) is designed with clarity in mind. Not only will you find clear explanations of what the Bible is saying but also unique insights into how you can apply God's eternal truths to daily living. The book of Mark is generally held to be the earliest account of the life of Jesus Christ. It clearly defines its purpose in the very first verse: "The beginning of the gospel about Jesus Christ, the Son of God" (Mark 1:1, NIV®). From there, the narrative presents a rapid, almost urgent look at the life of Jesus Christ. He is shown to be the Son of God with great power and authority.

Our Mission

The mission of WordTruth Press is to provide quality Bible-based resources with significant spiritual impact for individuals and churches. Education and evangelism are the main focus of WordTruth Press. Following the Great Commission of the LORD Jesus[2] this organization provides Bible-based resources to evangelize the world, encourage and equip believers and churches for evangelism, and provide solid Bible teaching to build up the body of Christ.

A key strategy is to find low-cost channels for production and distribution to maximize the availability of our resources to people around the world. WordTruth Press also offers many free resources for churches and individuals available online at WordTruthPress.Org.

---

[2] Matthew 28:18-20.

Made in the USA
Columbia, SC
28 July 2021